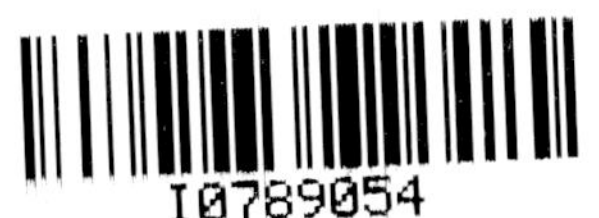

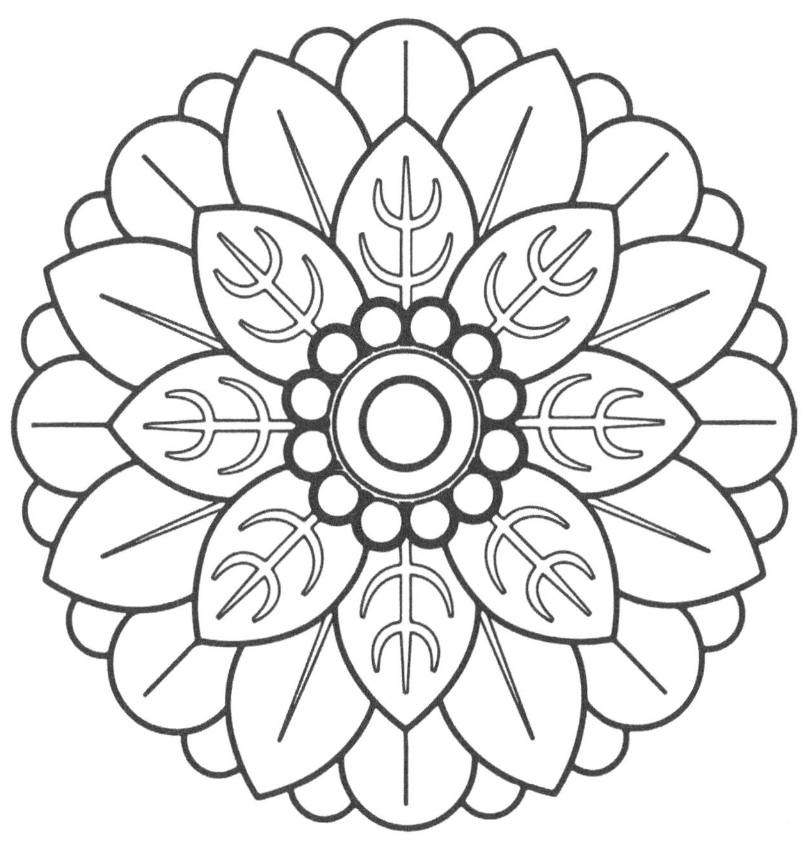

Easy Mandala coloring book

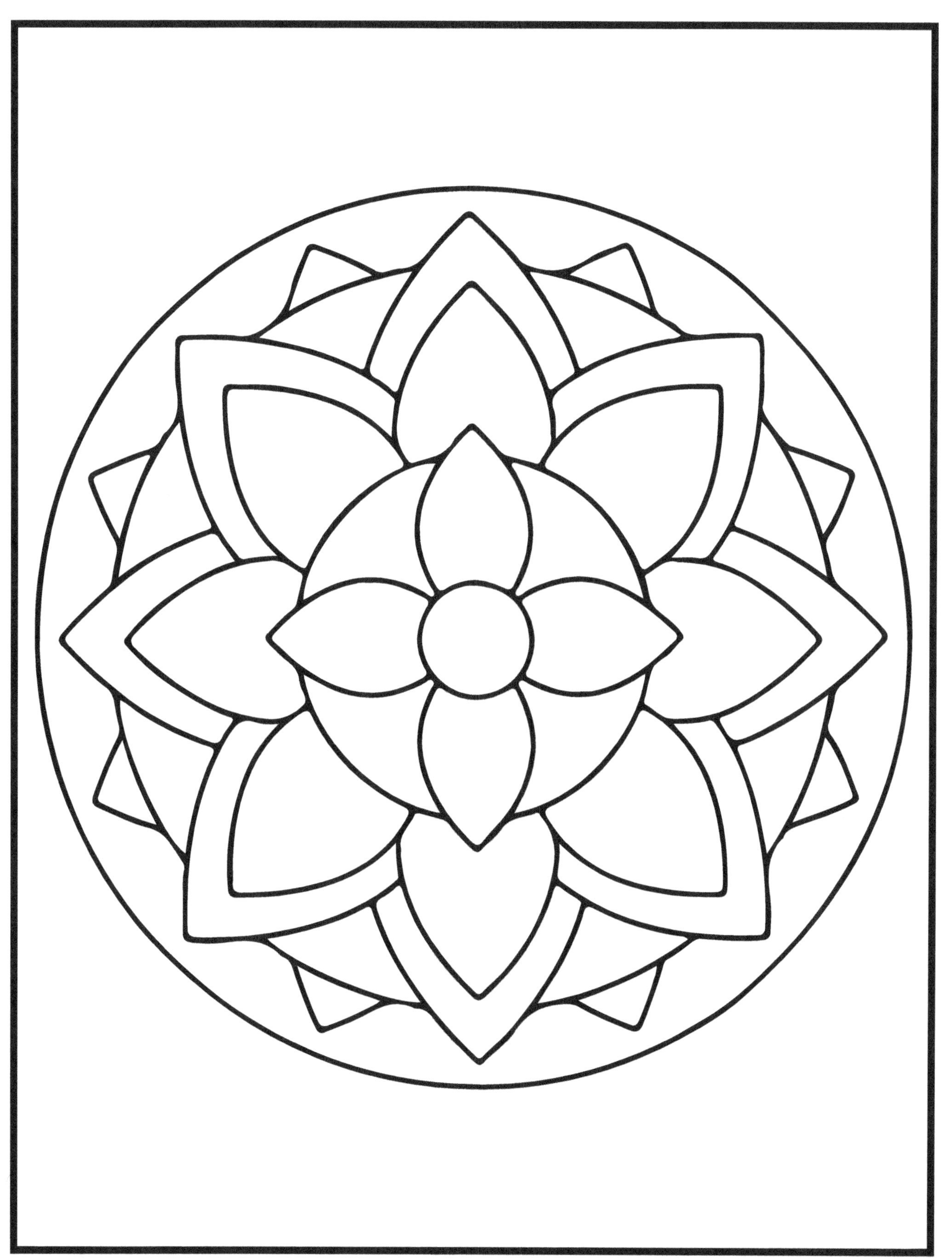

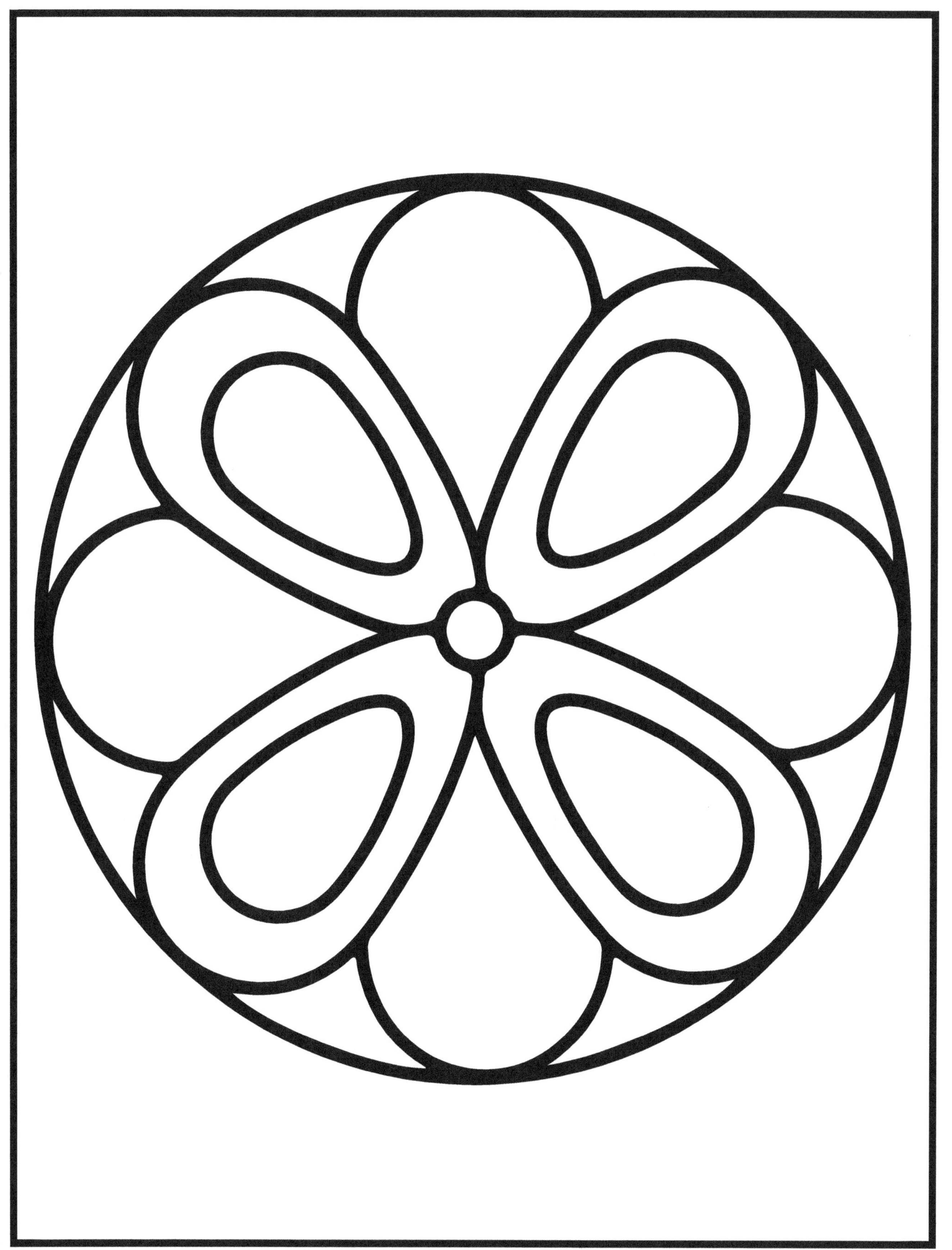

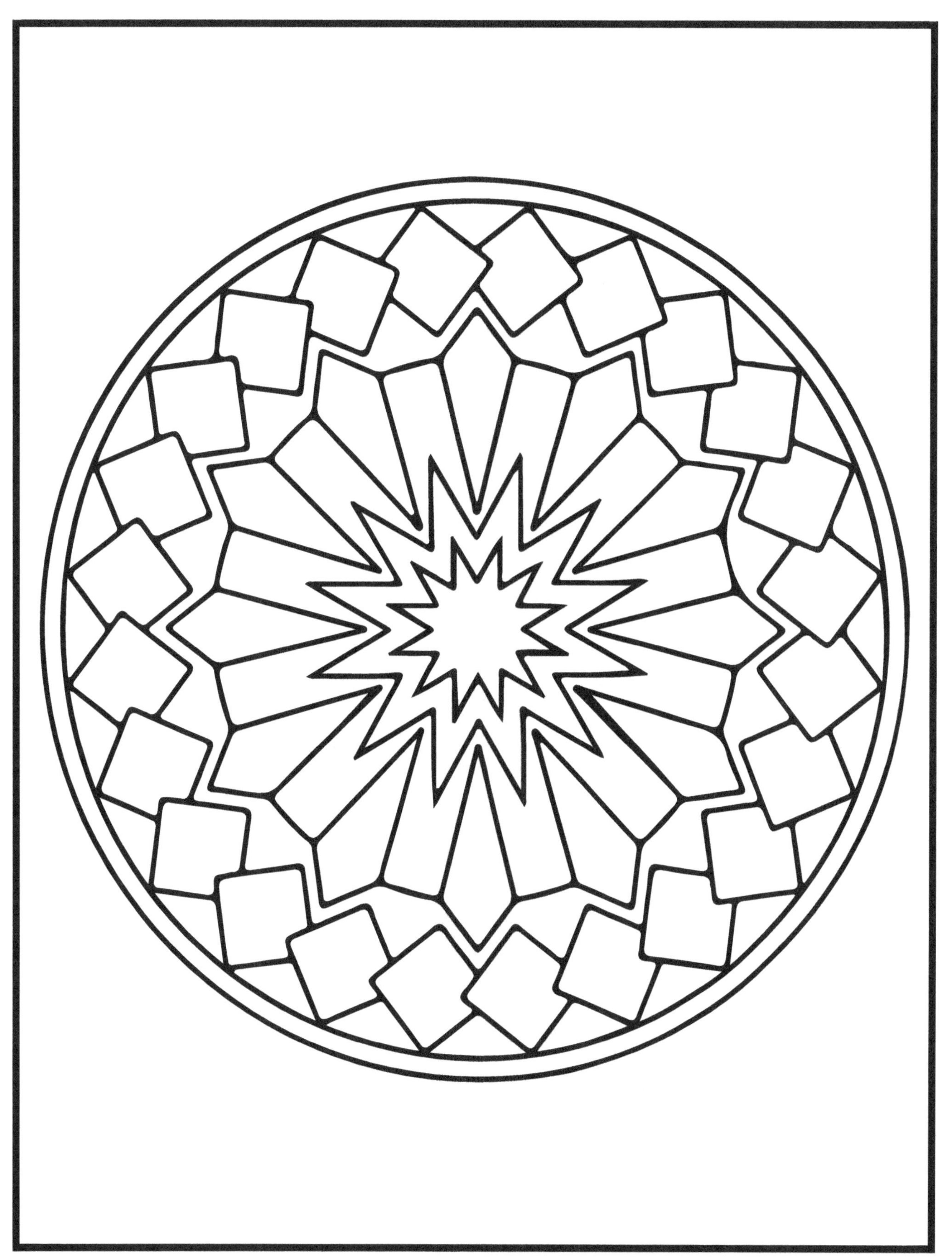

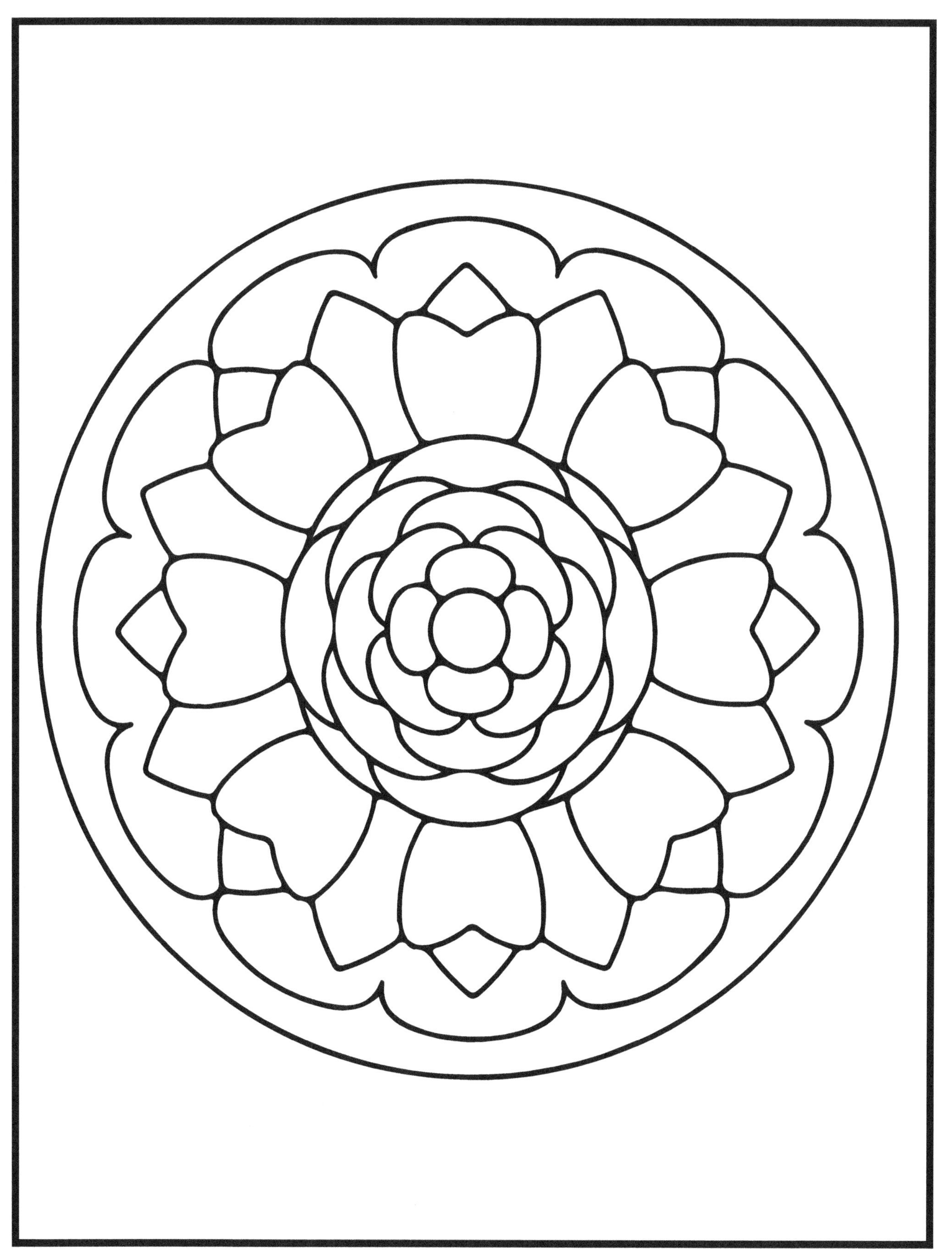

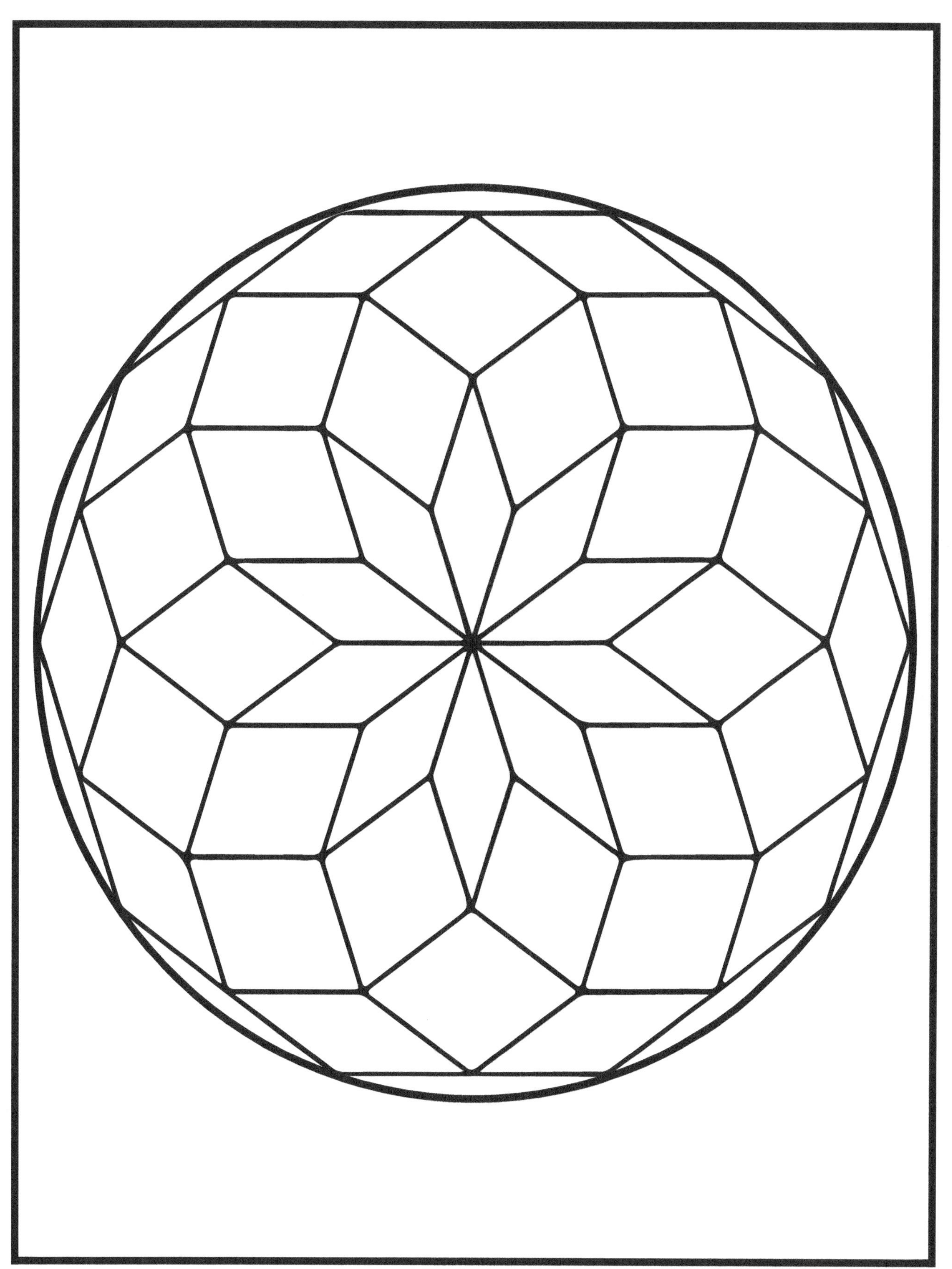

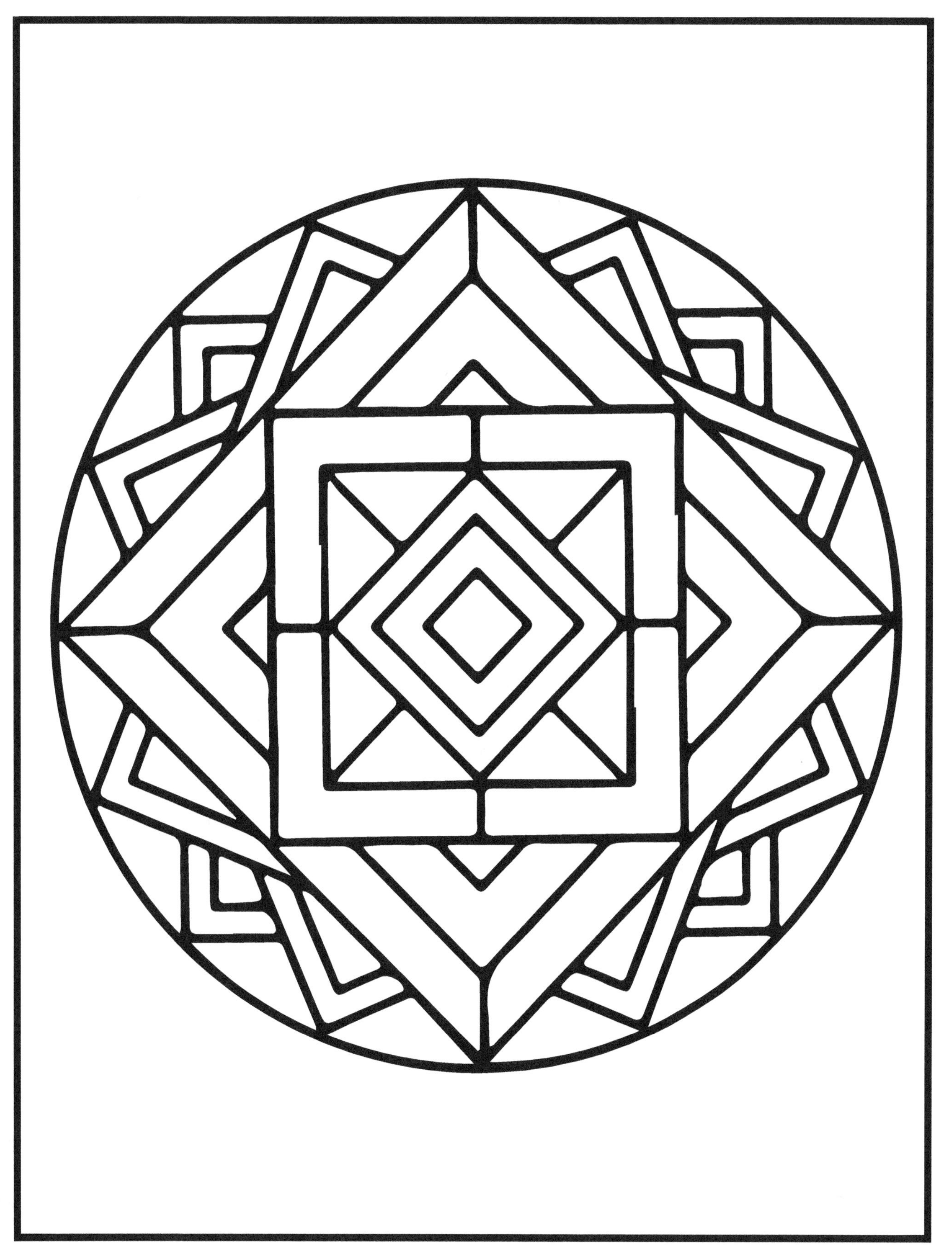

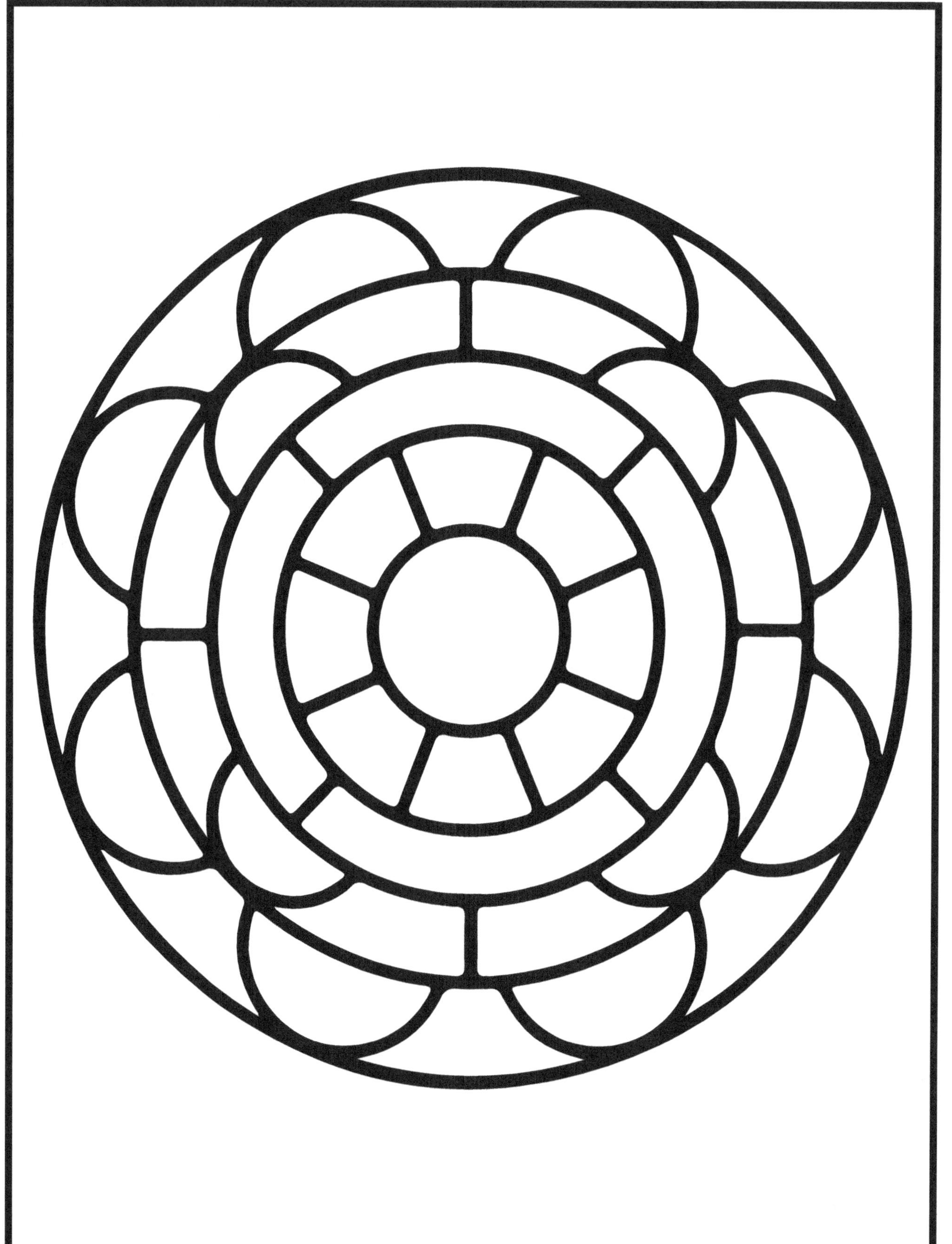

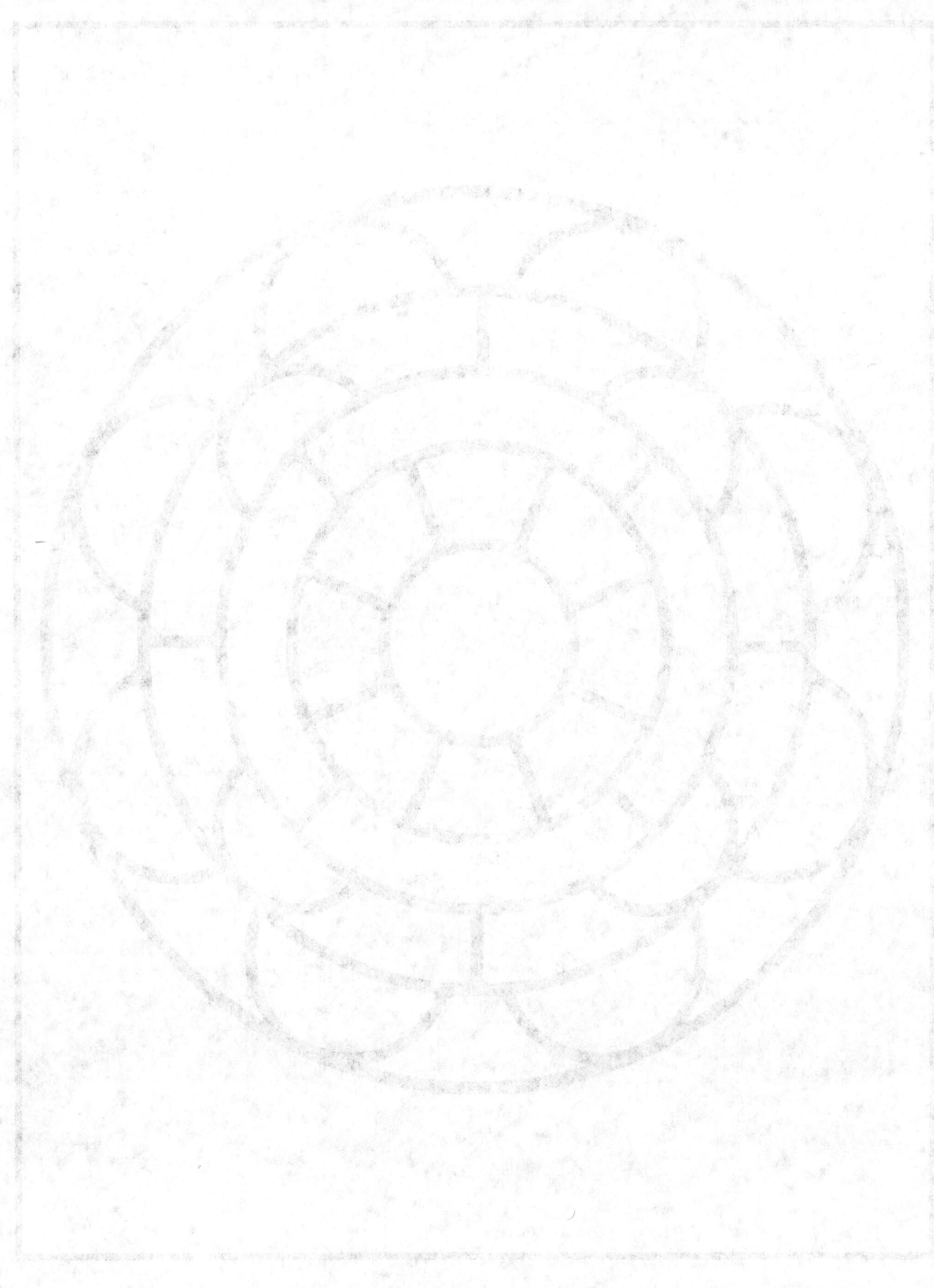

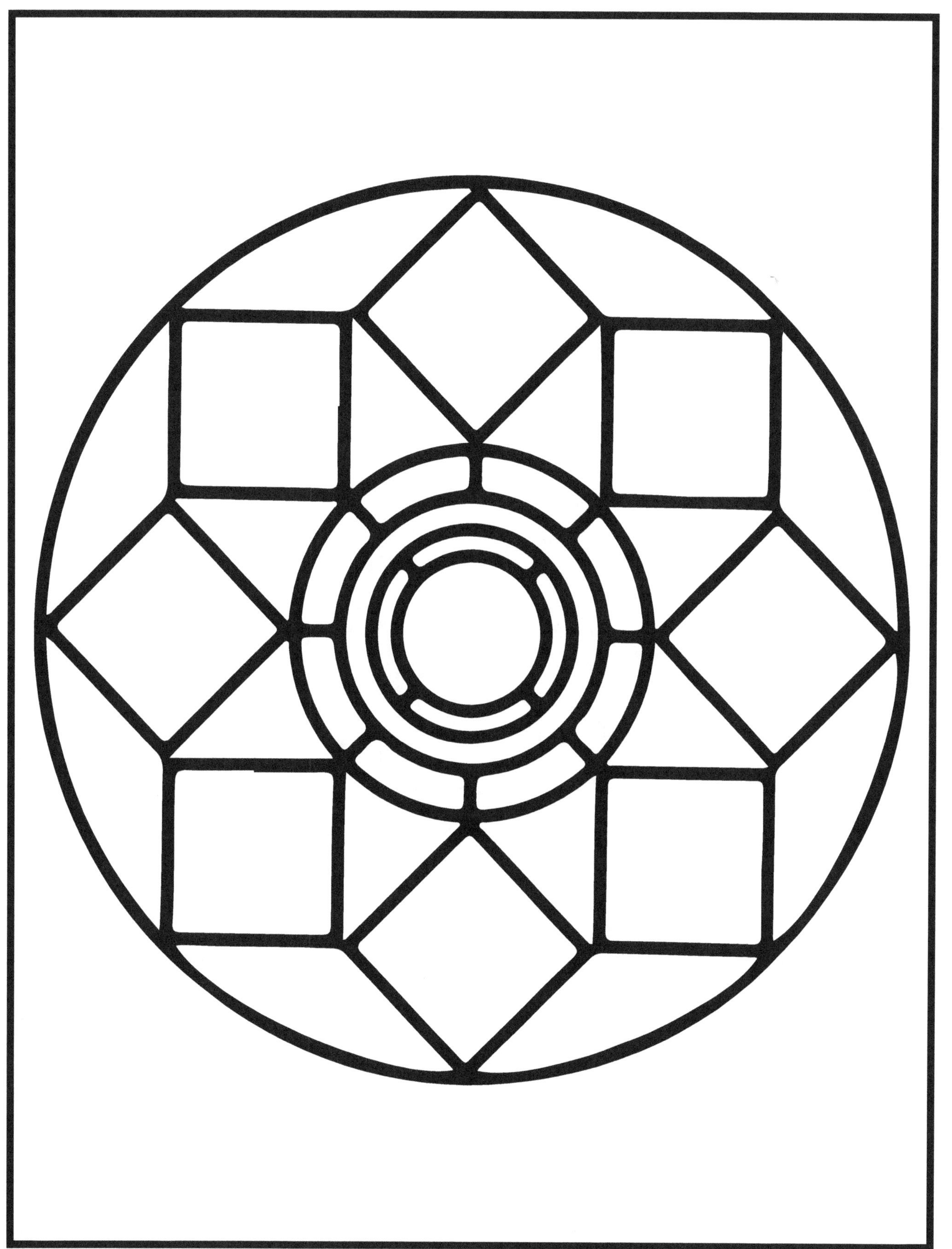

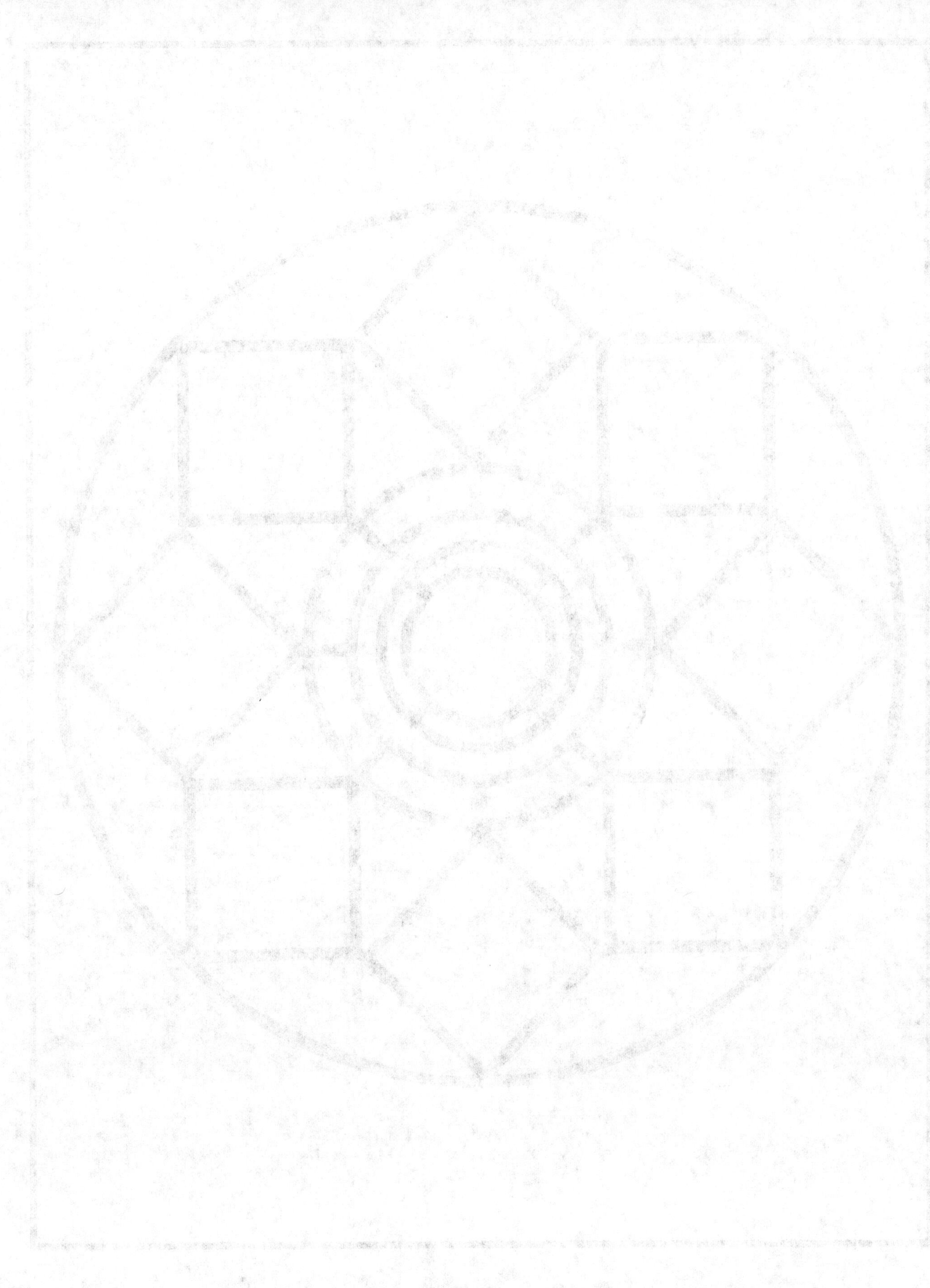

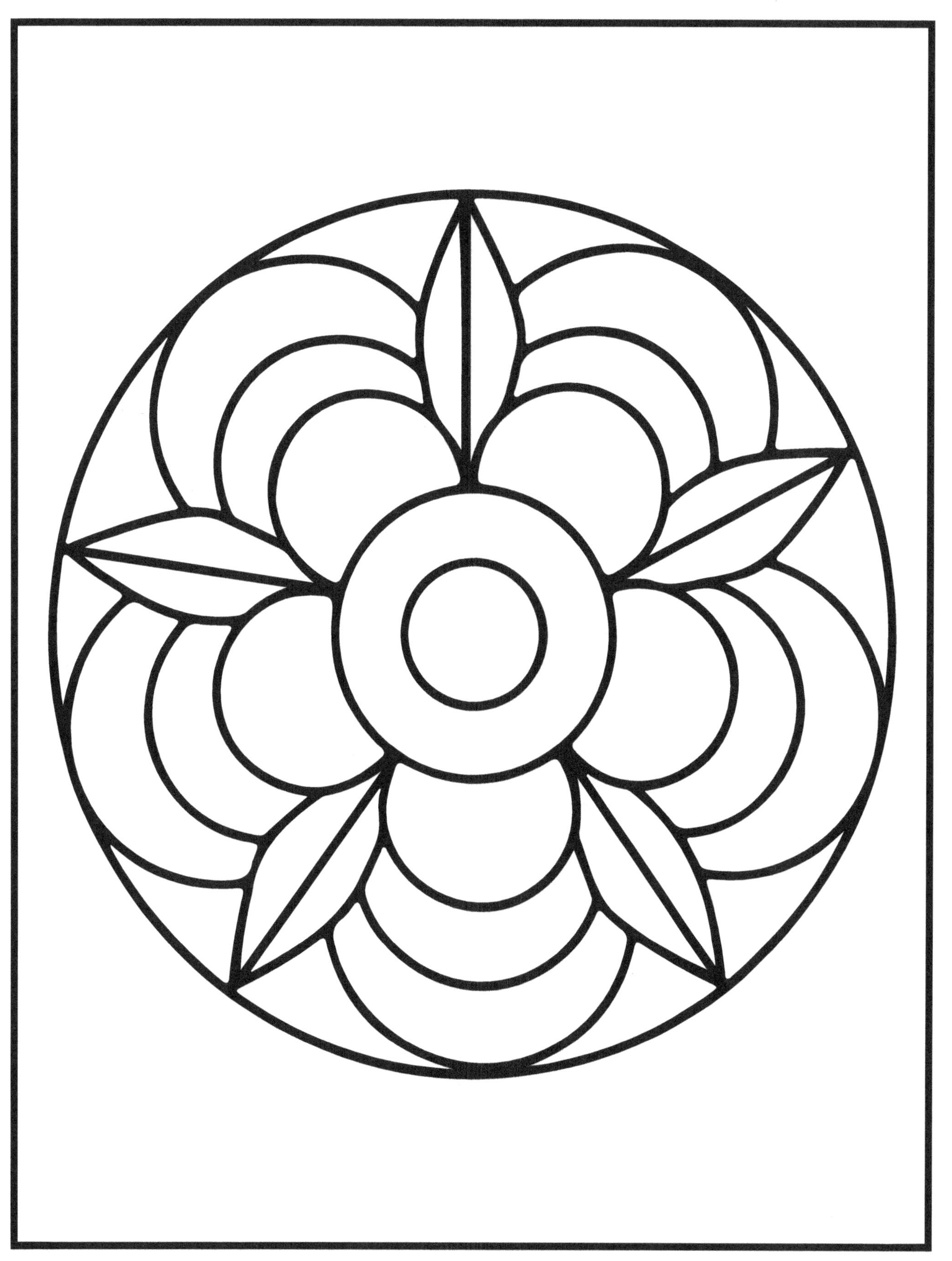

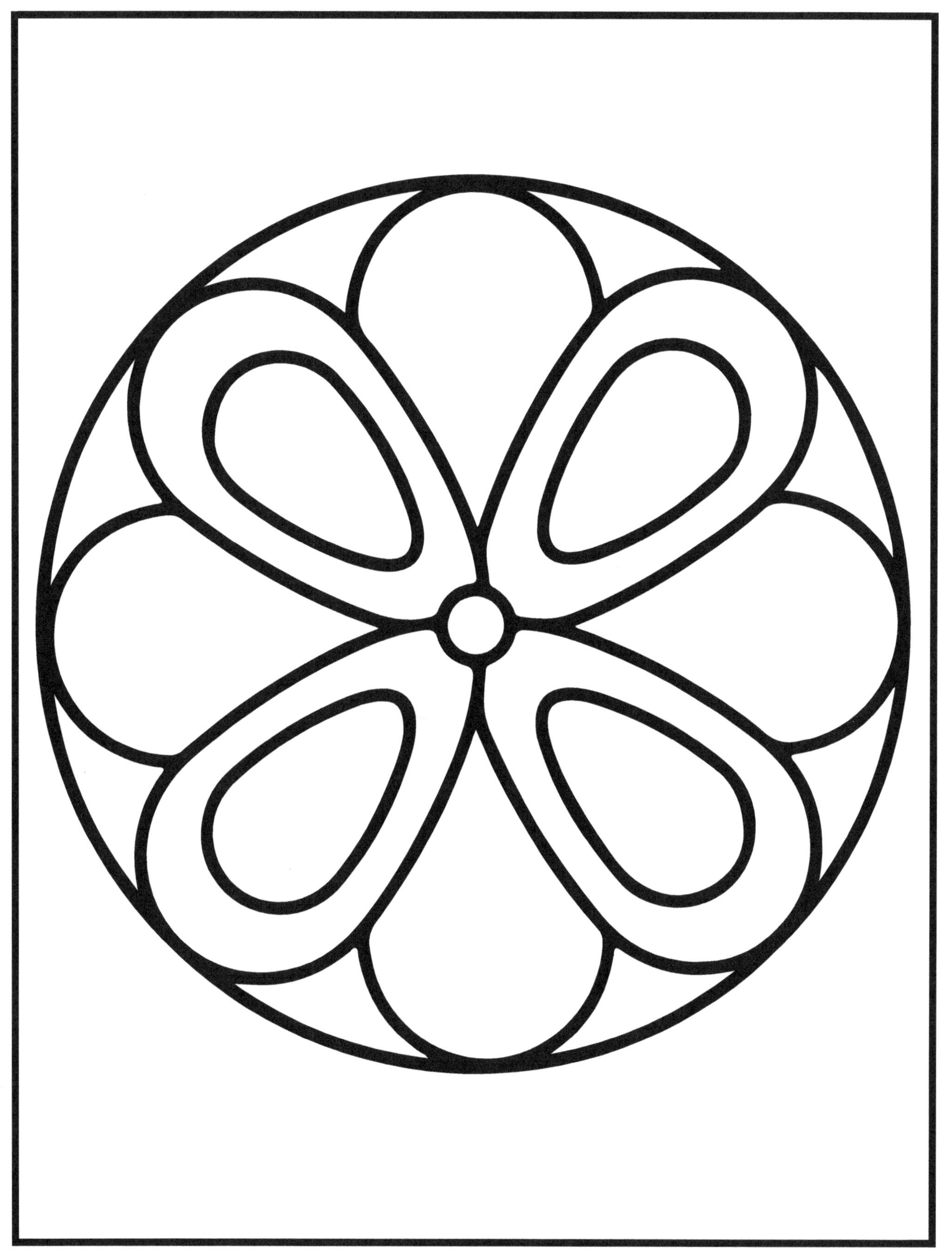

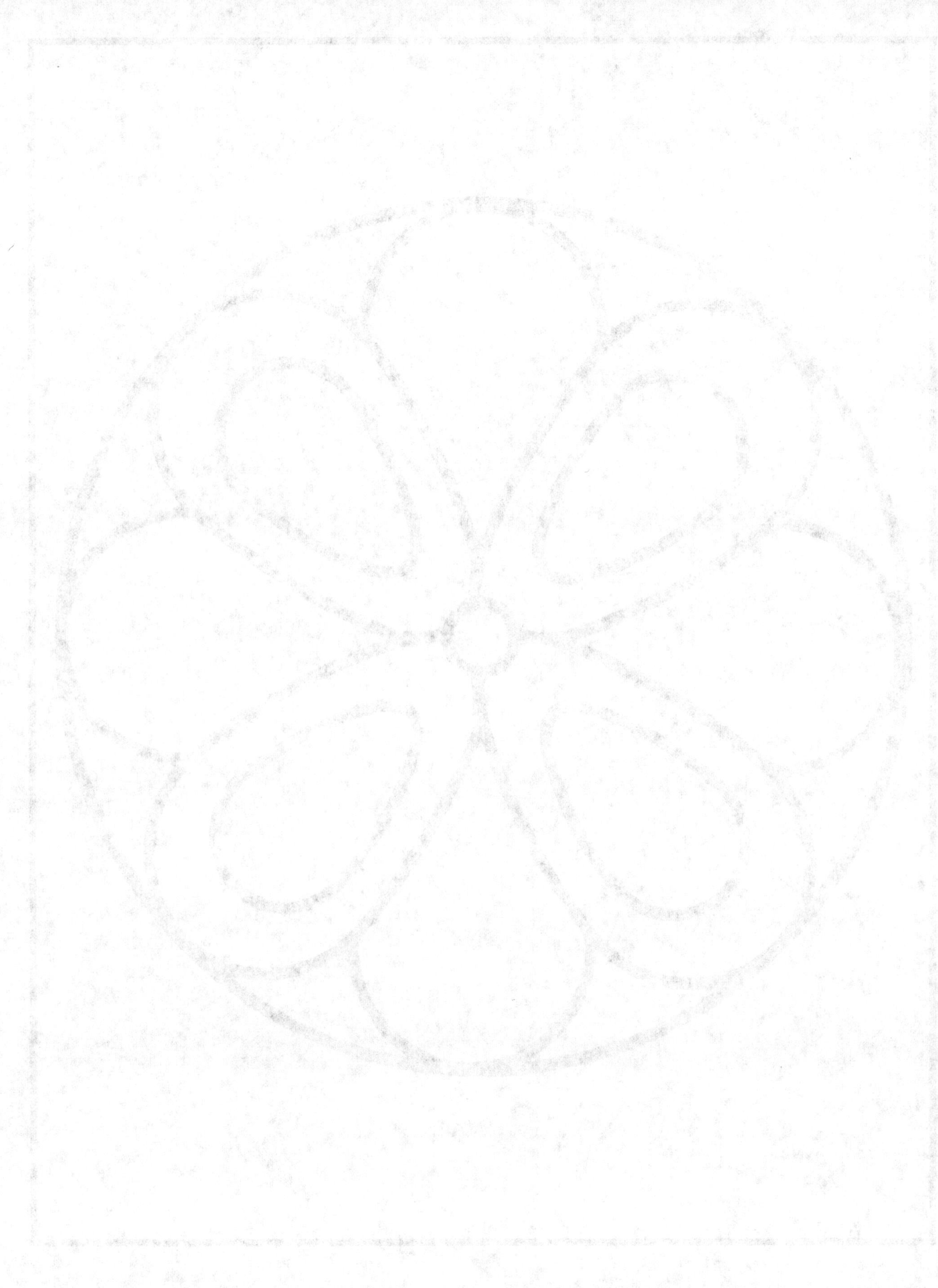

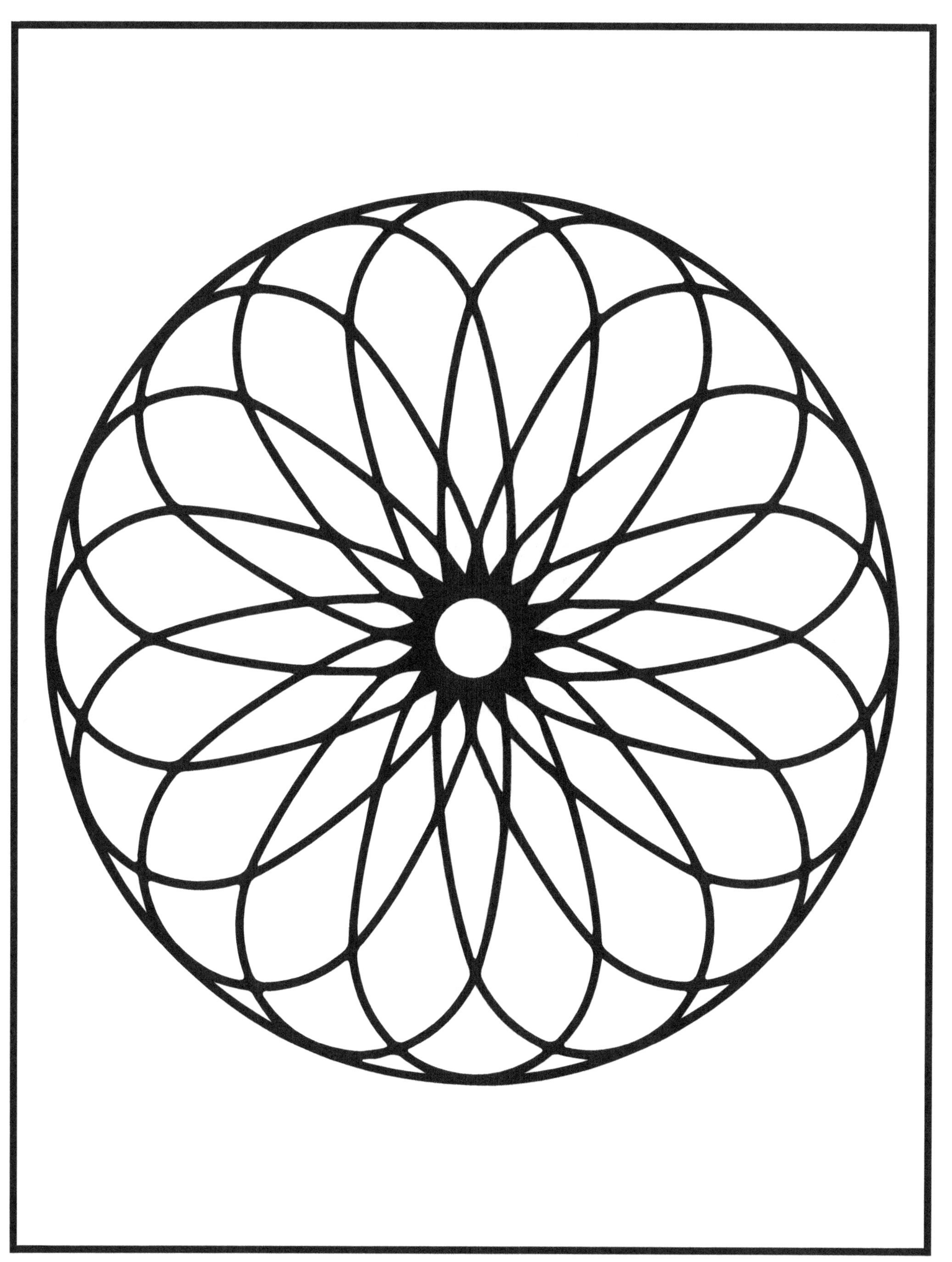

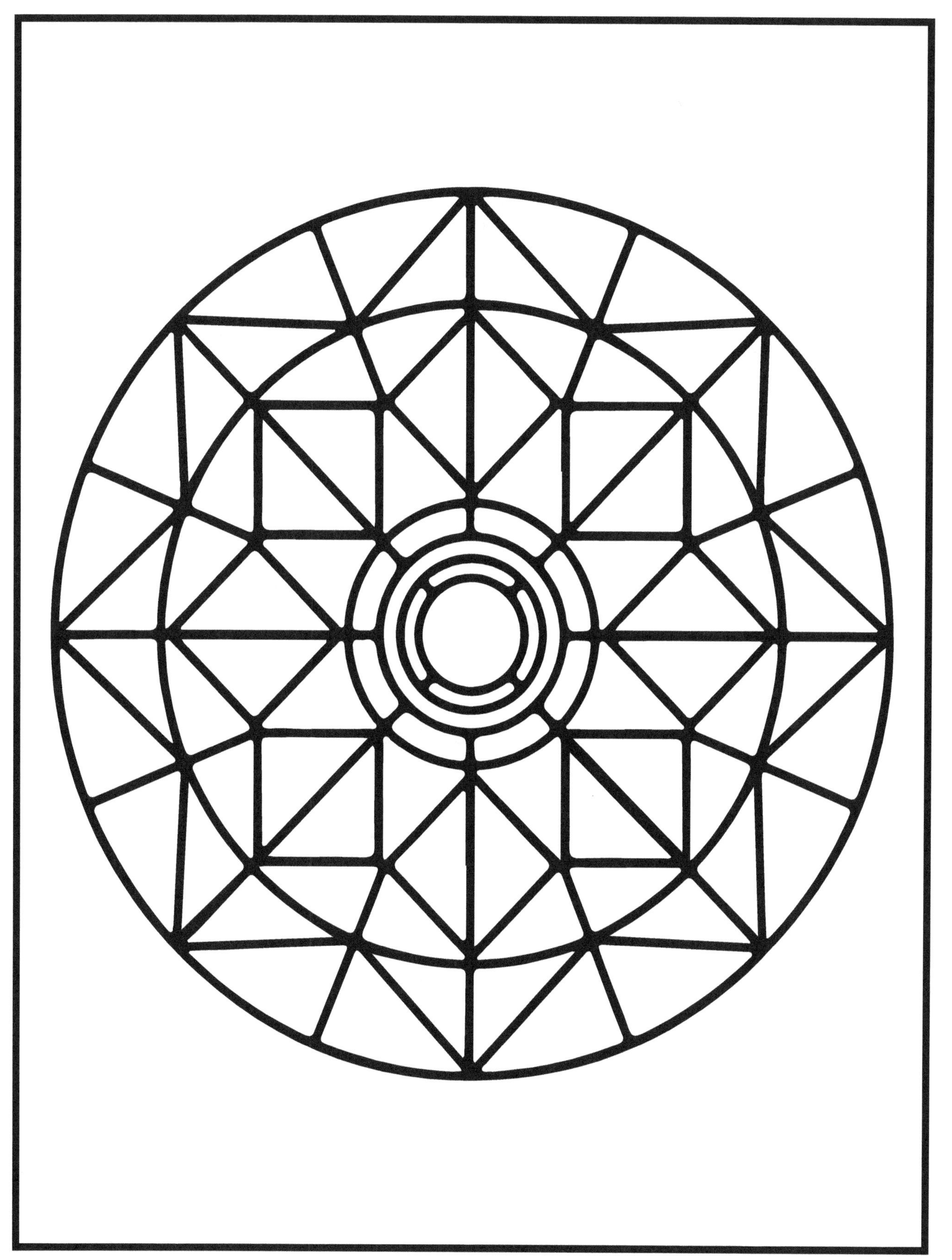

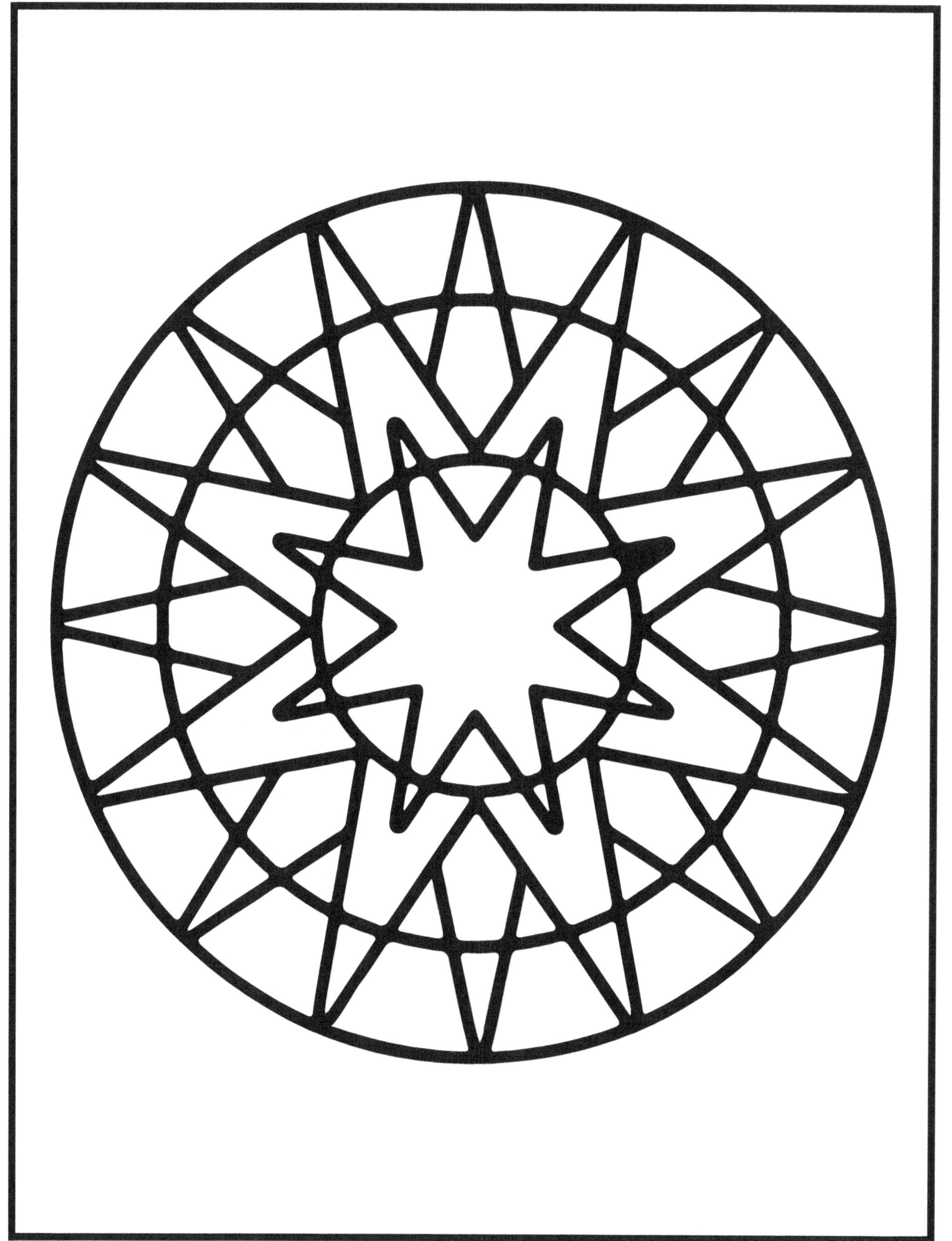

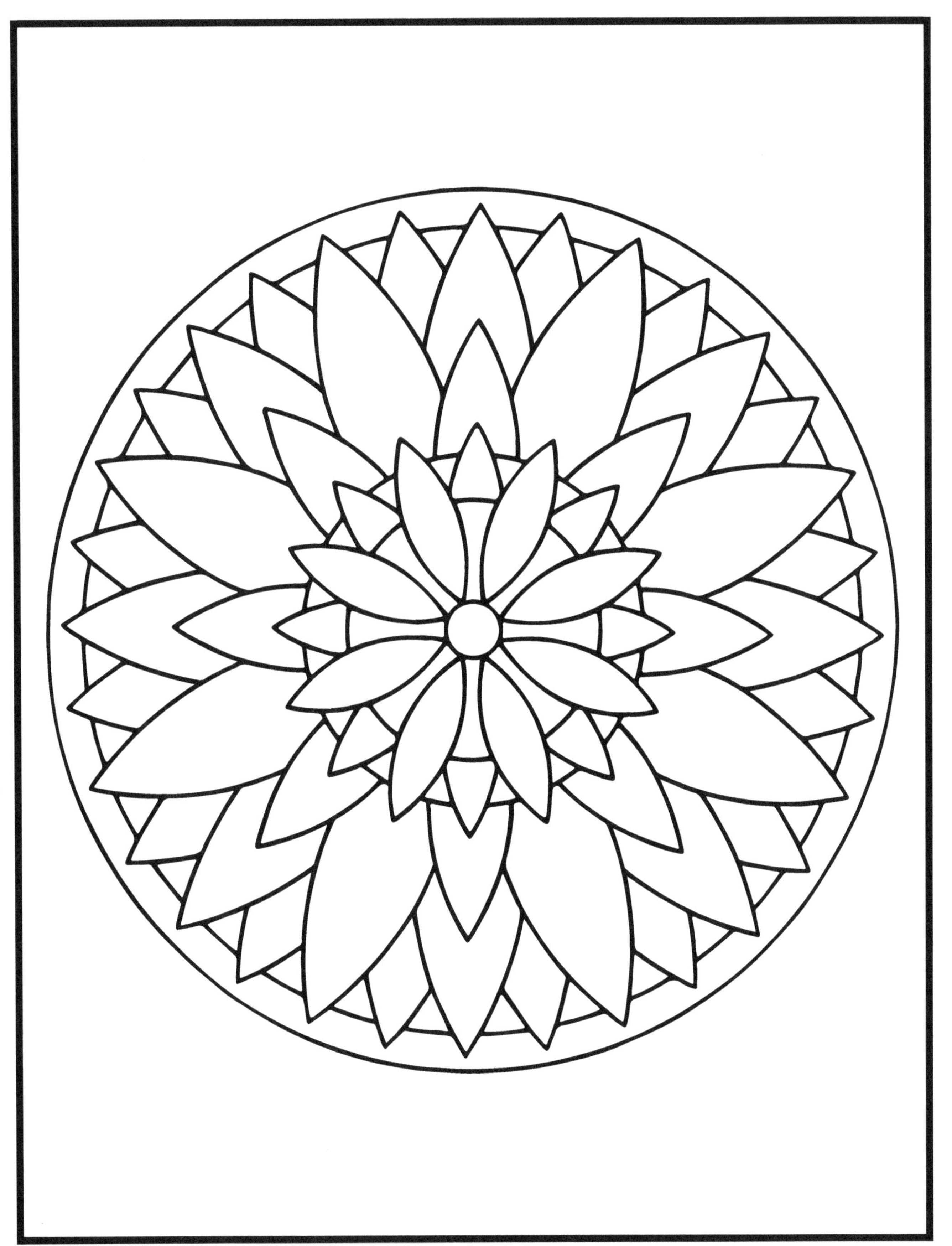

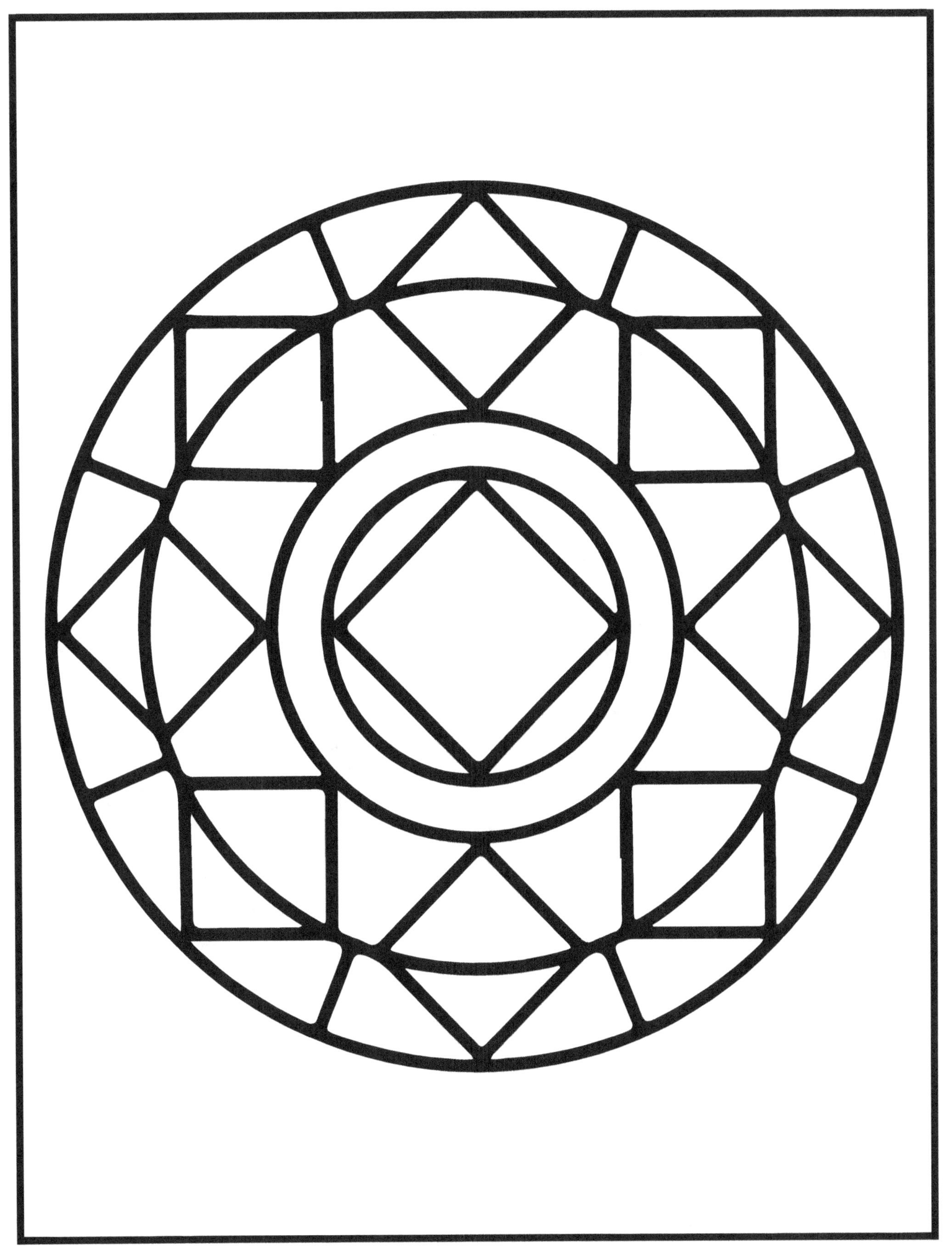

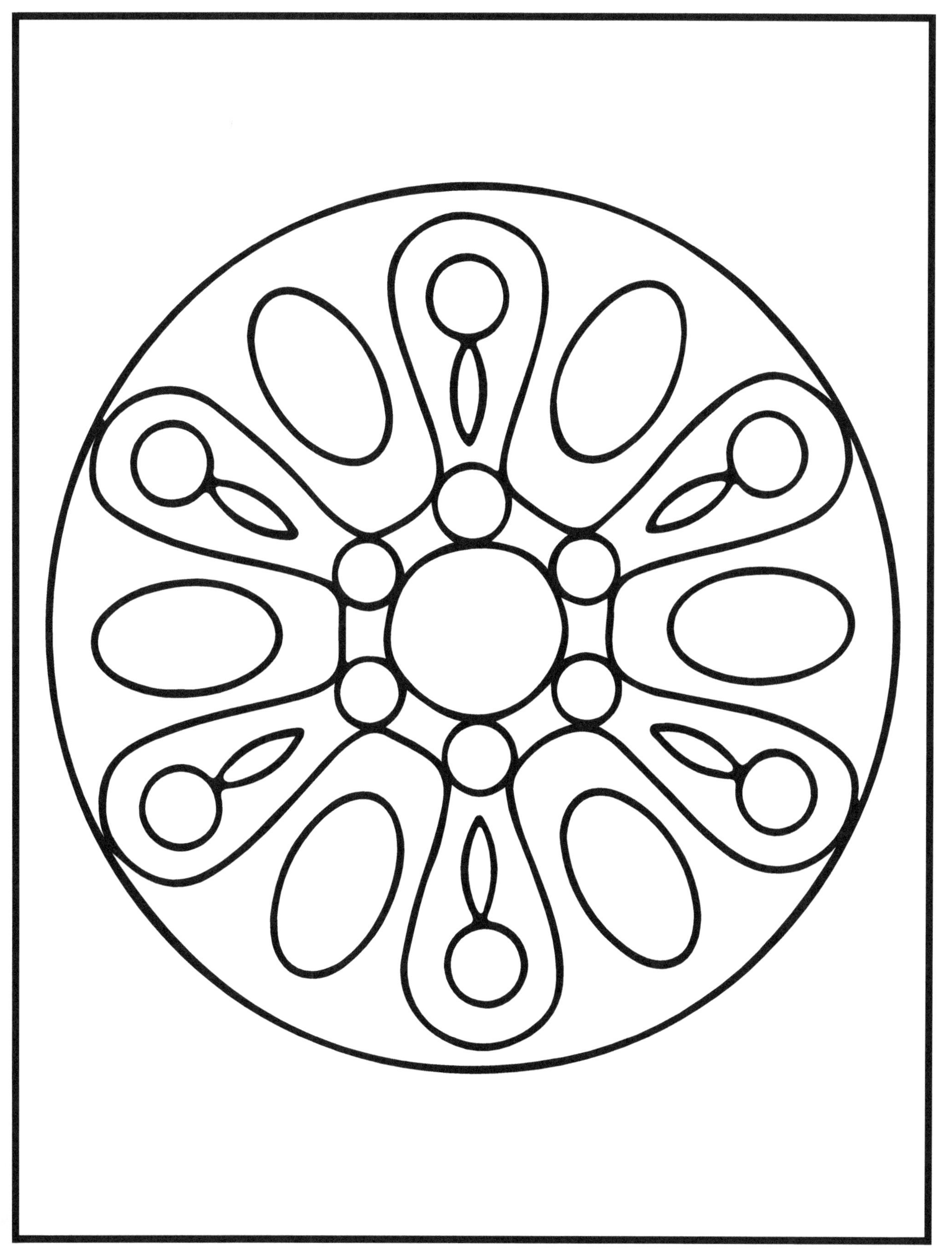

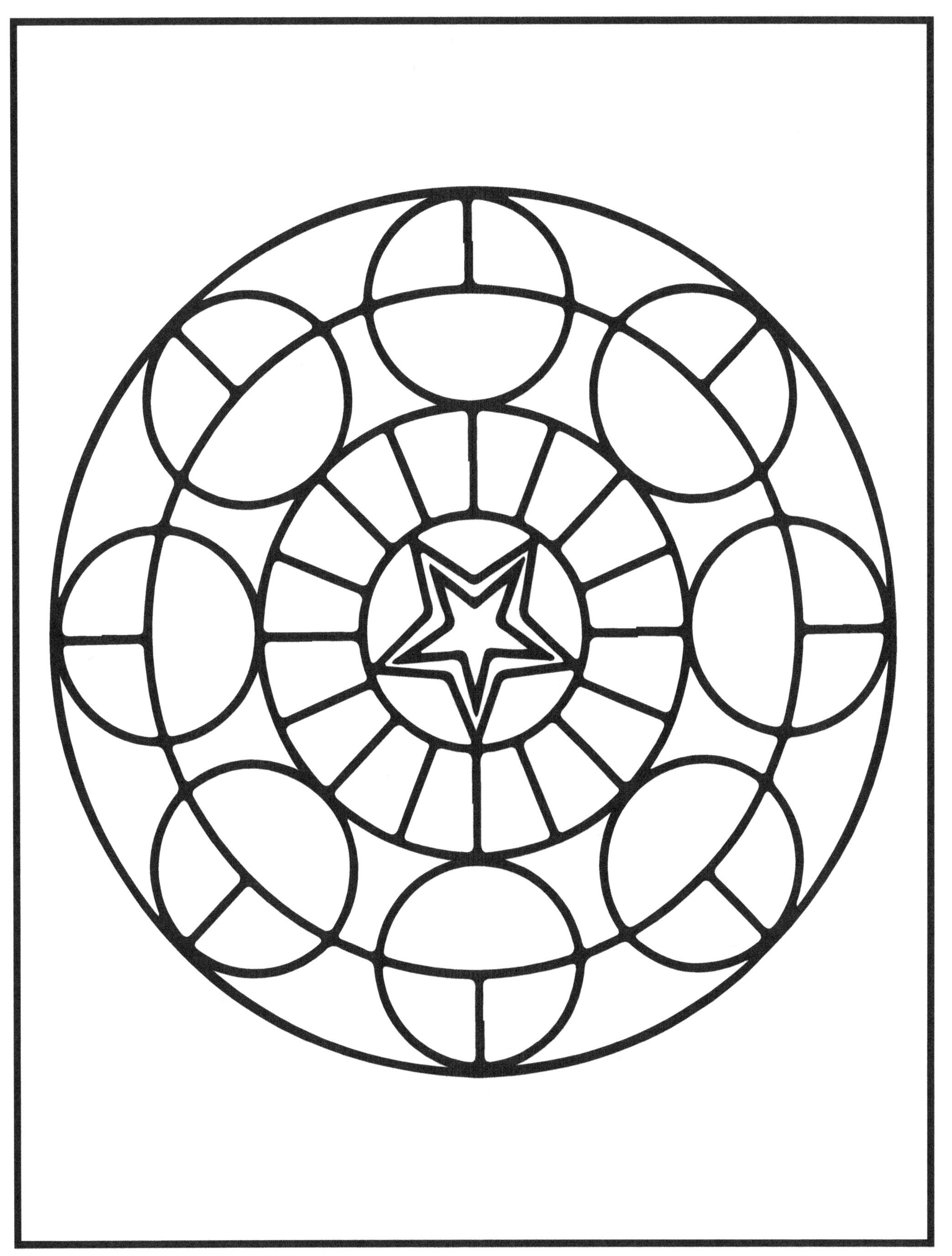

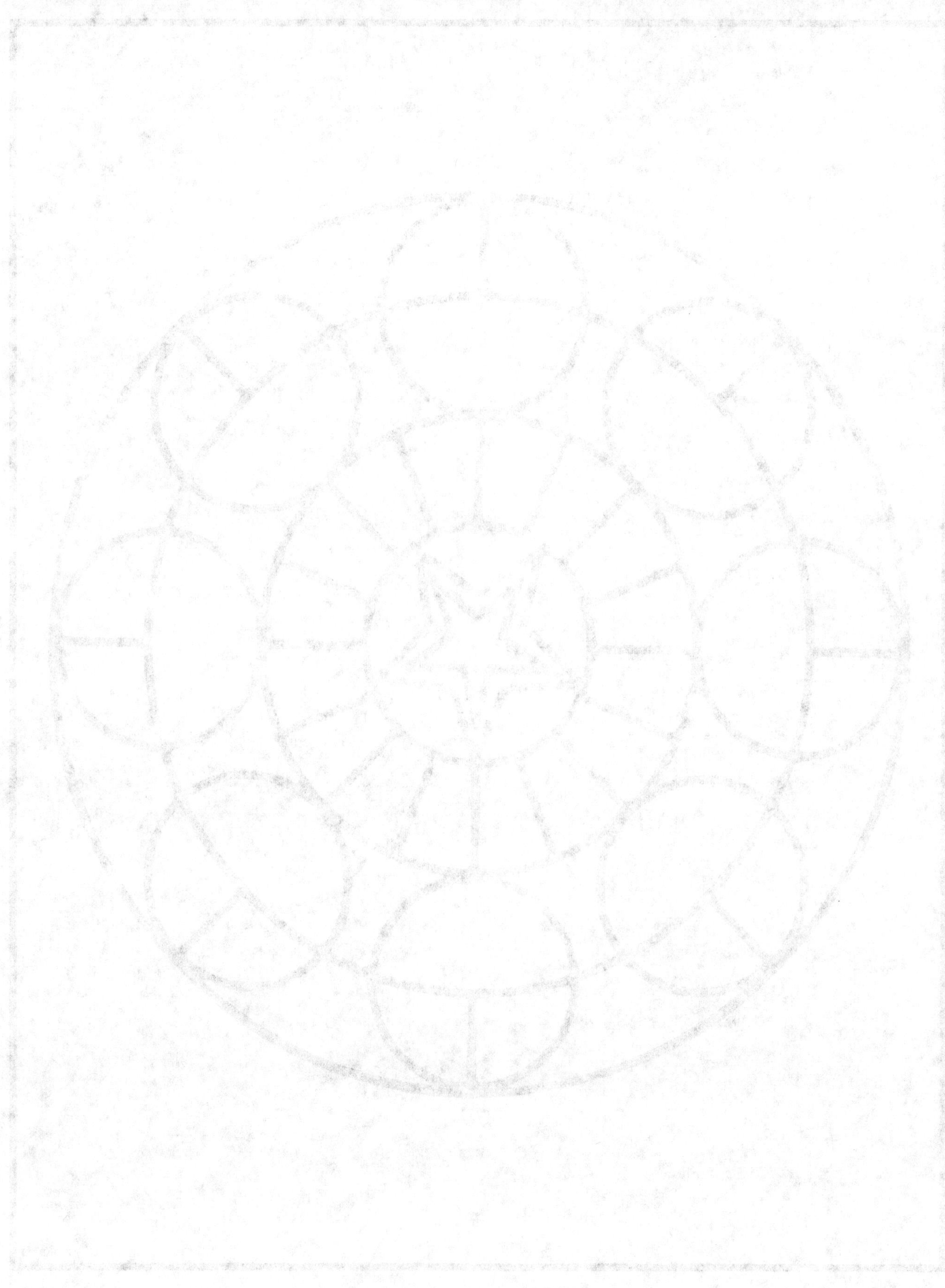

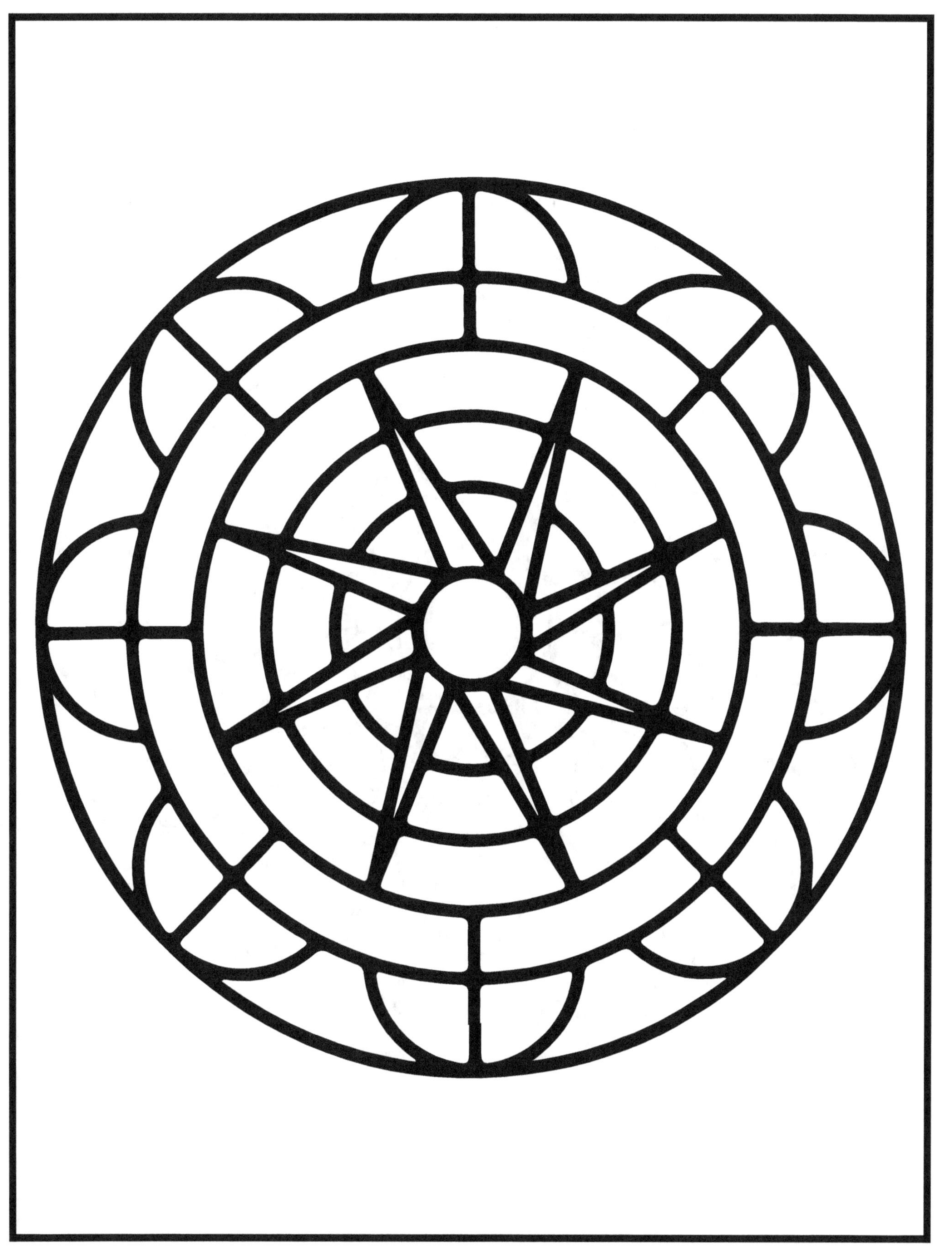

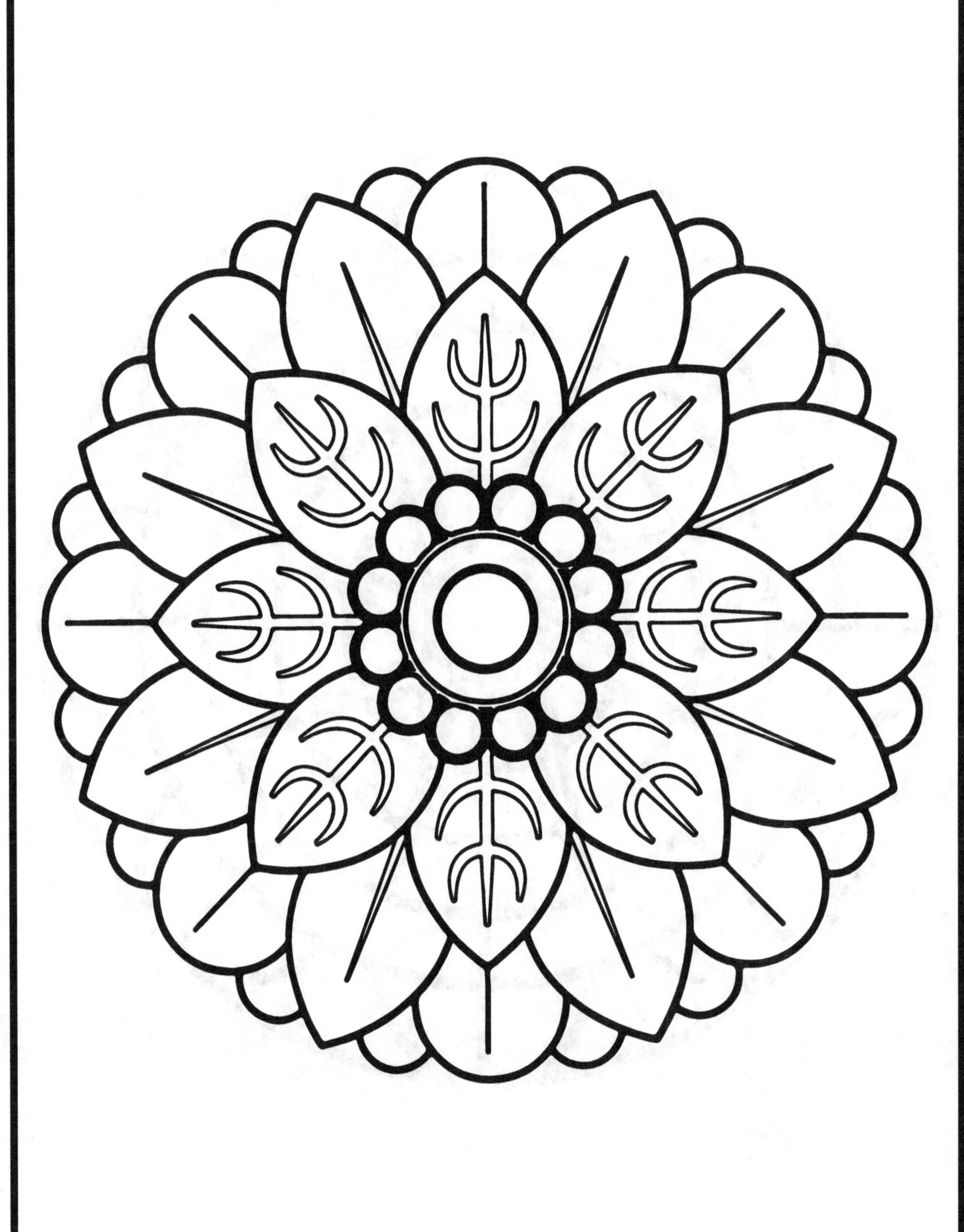

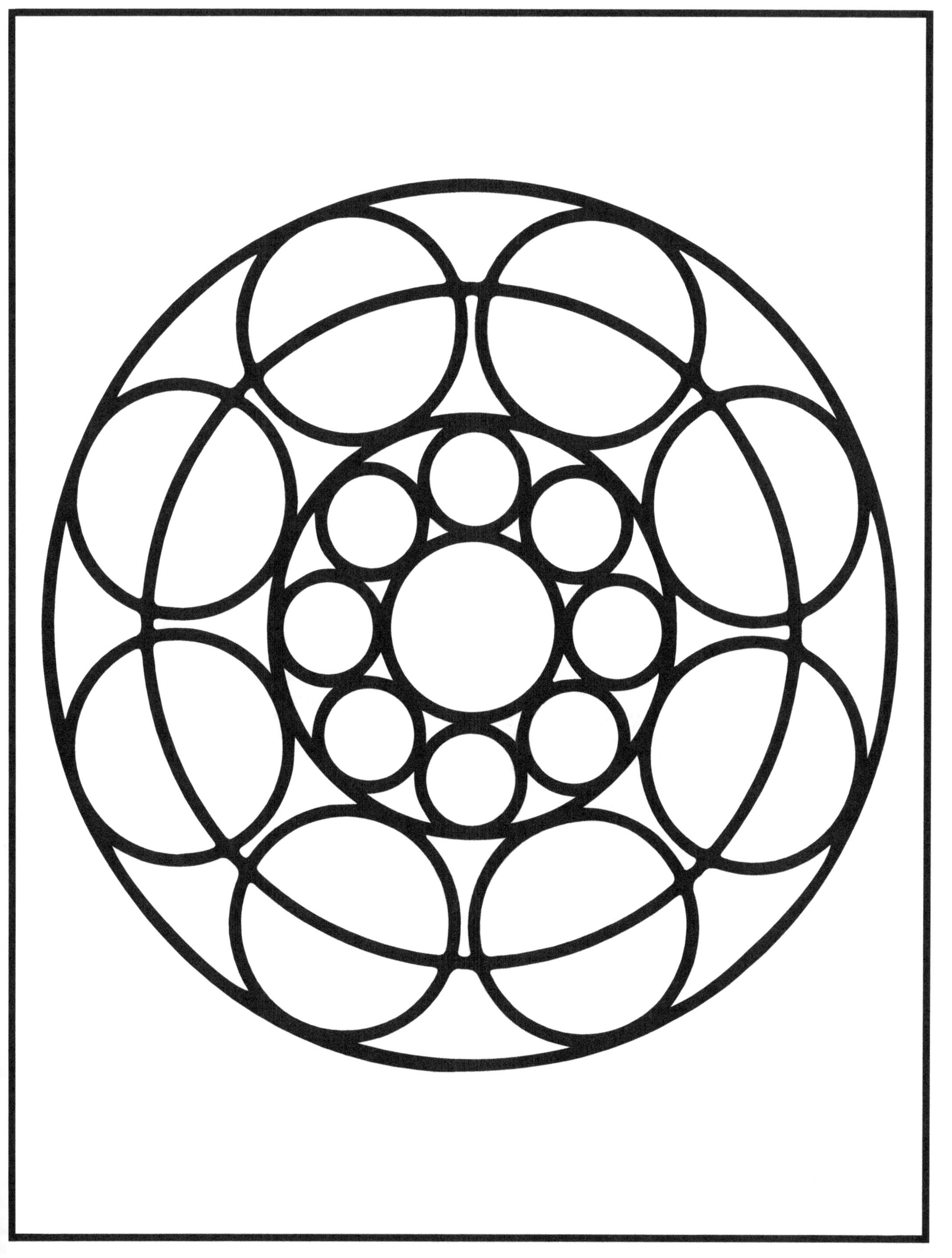

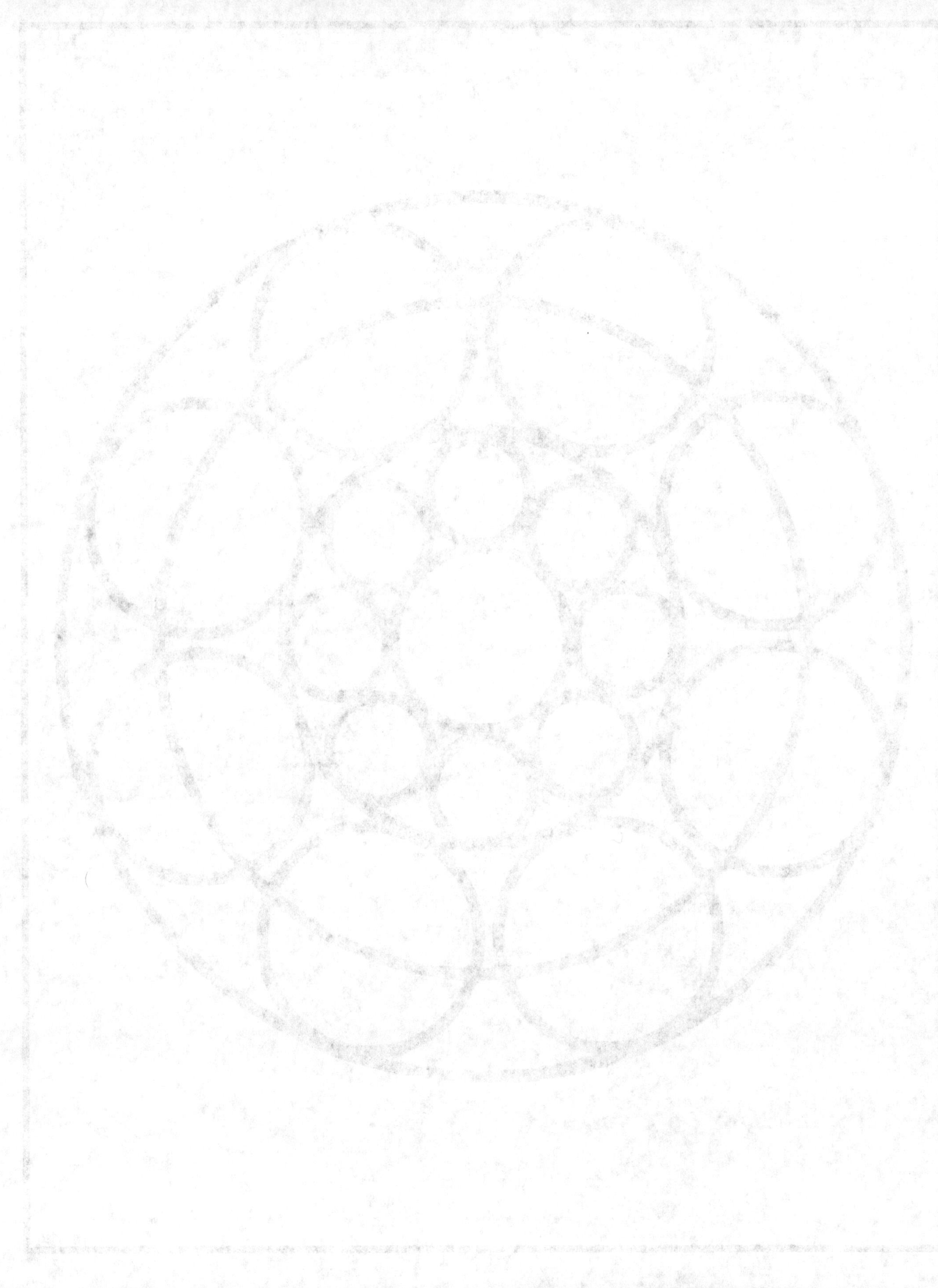

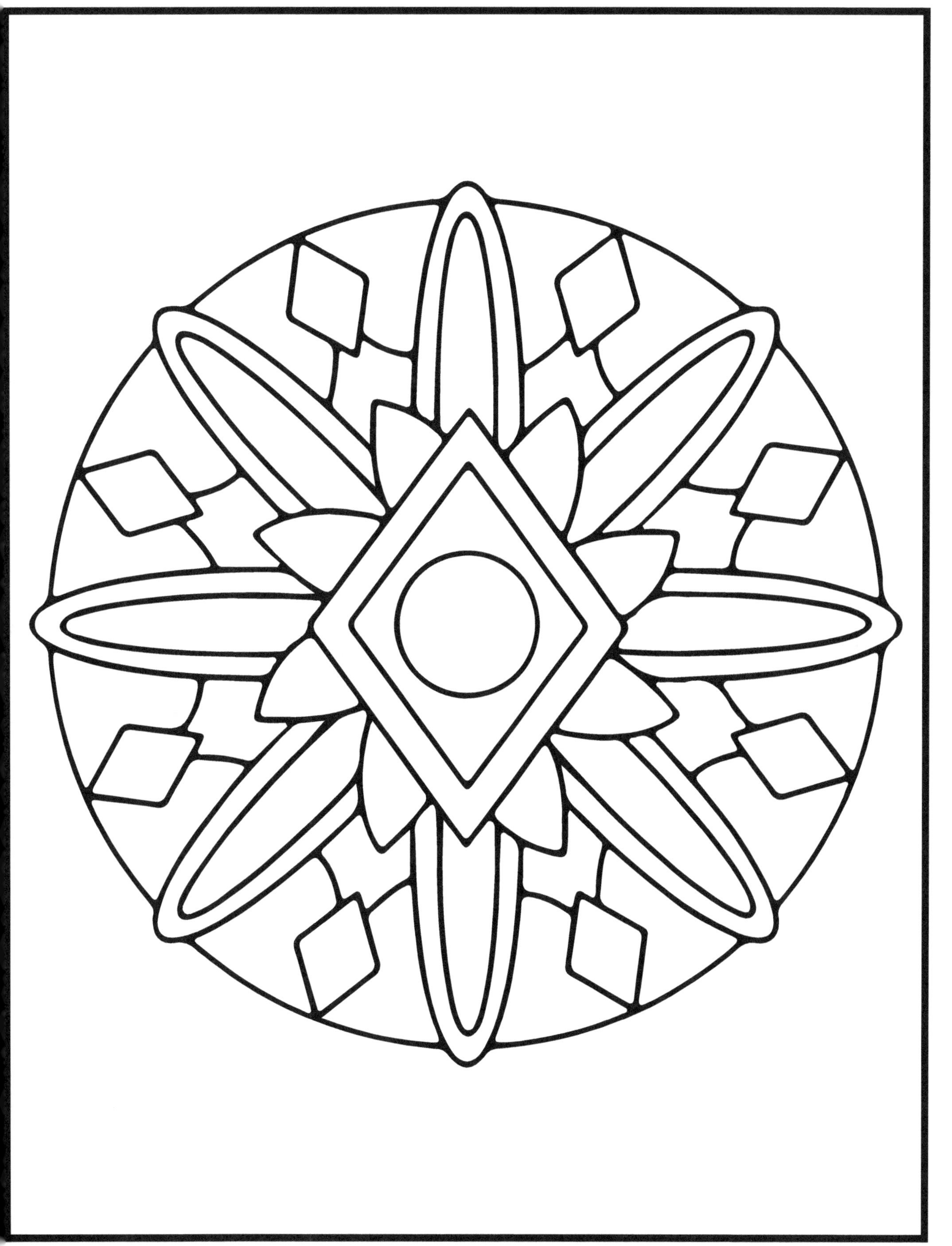

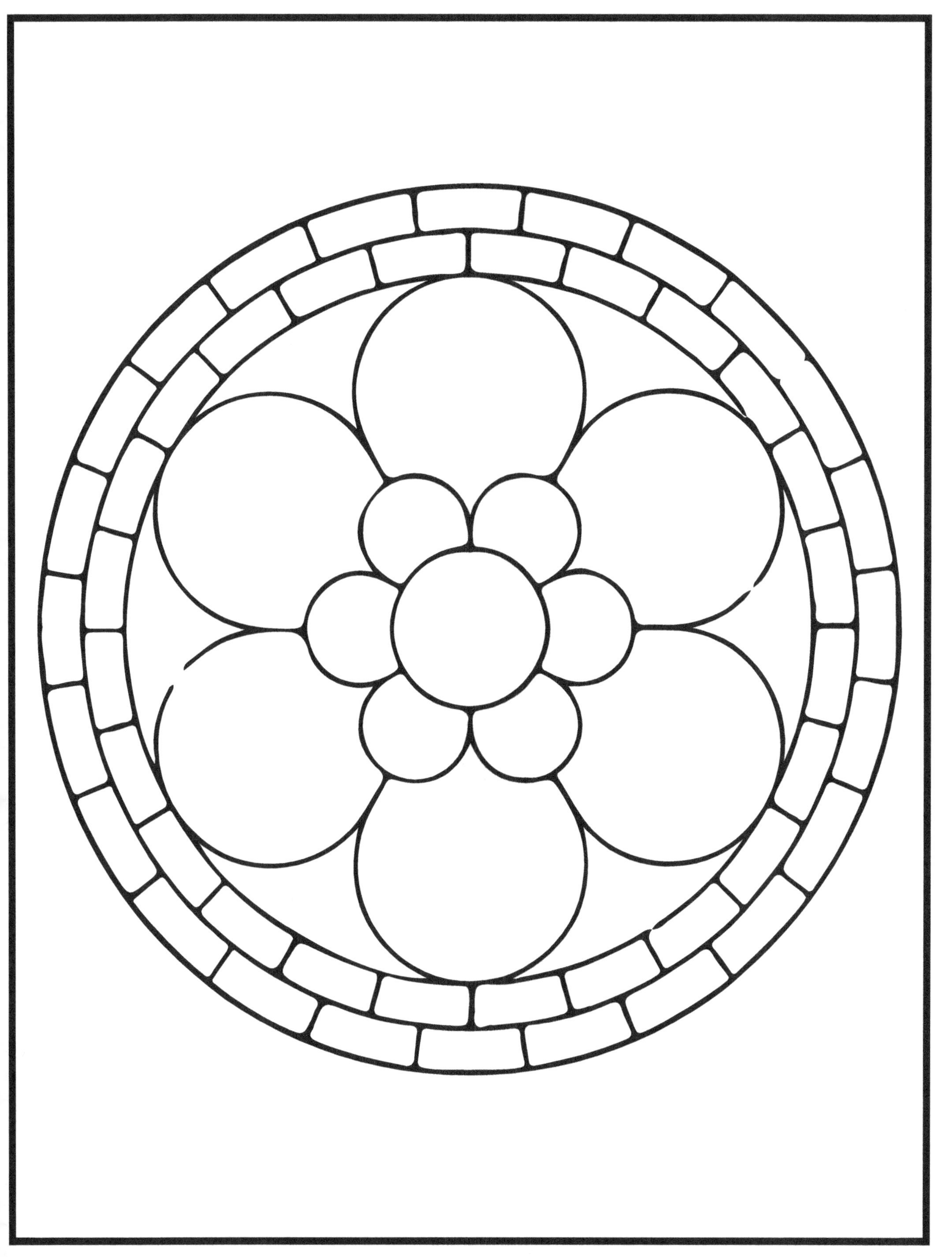

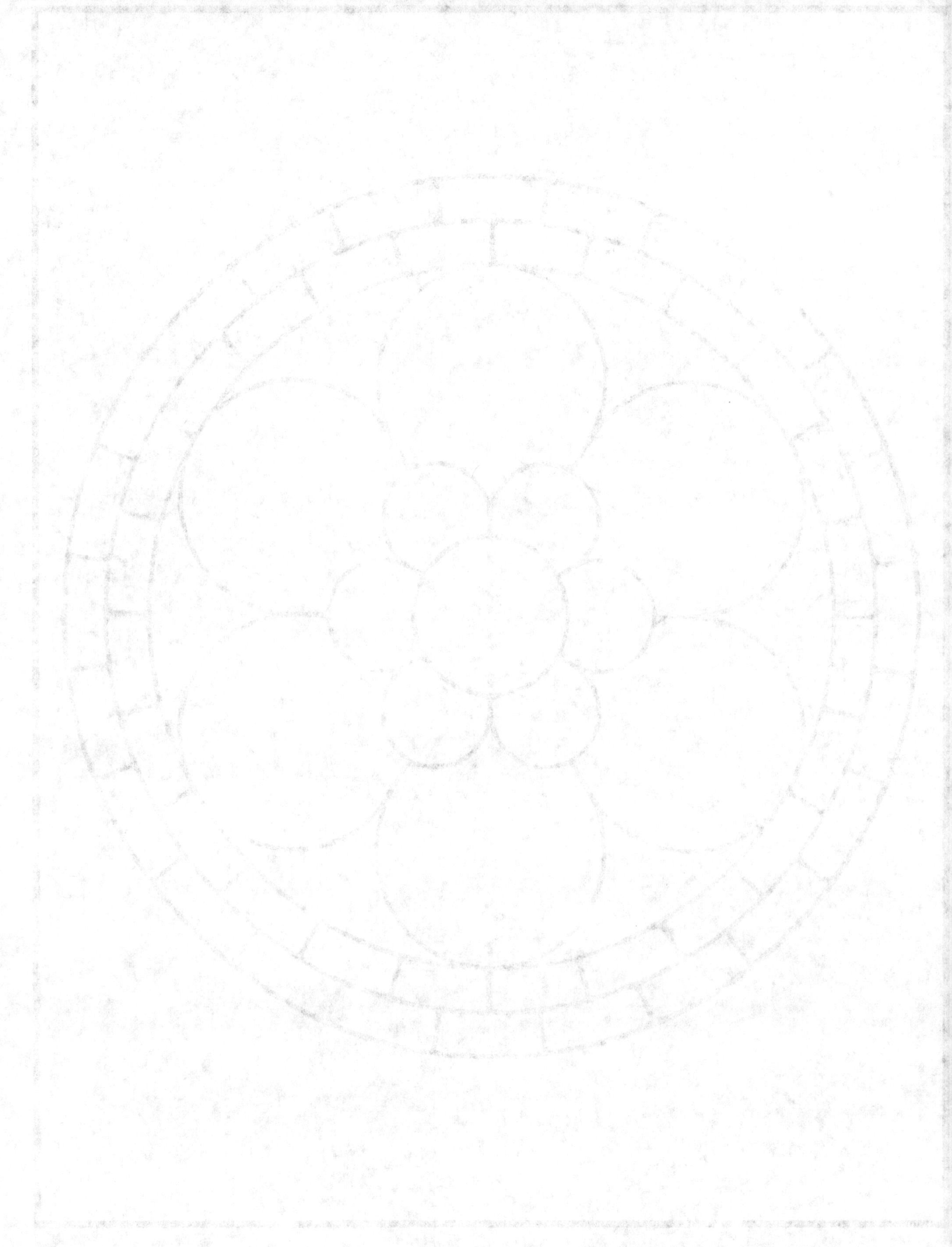

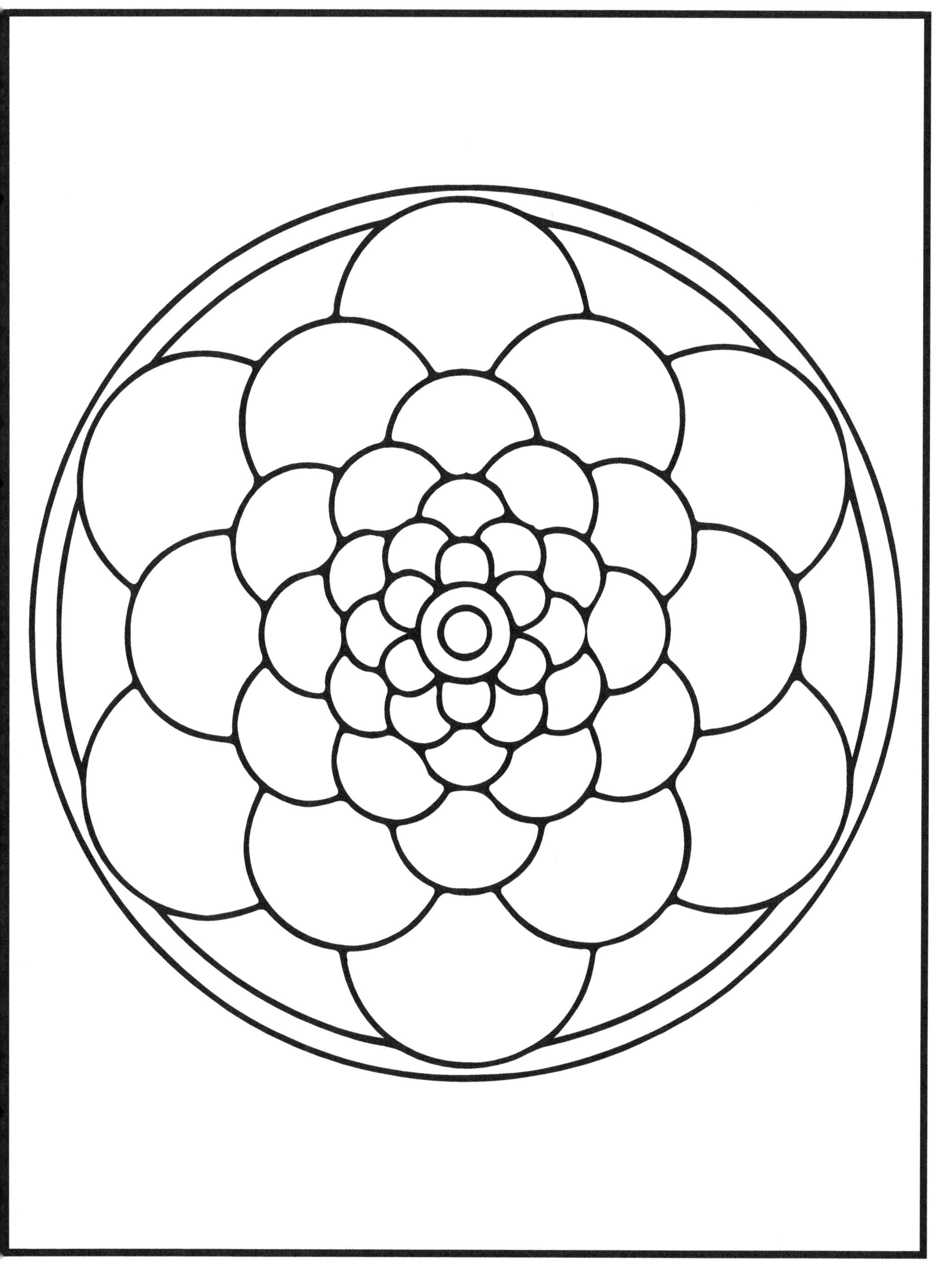

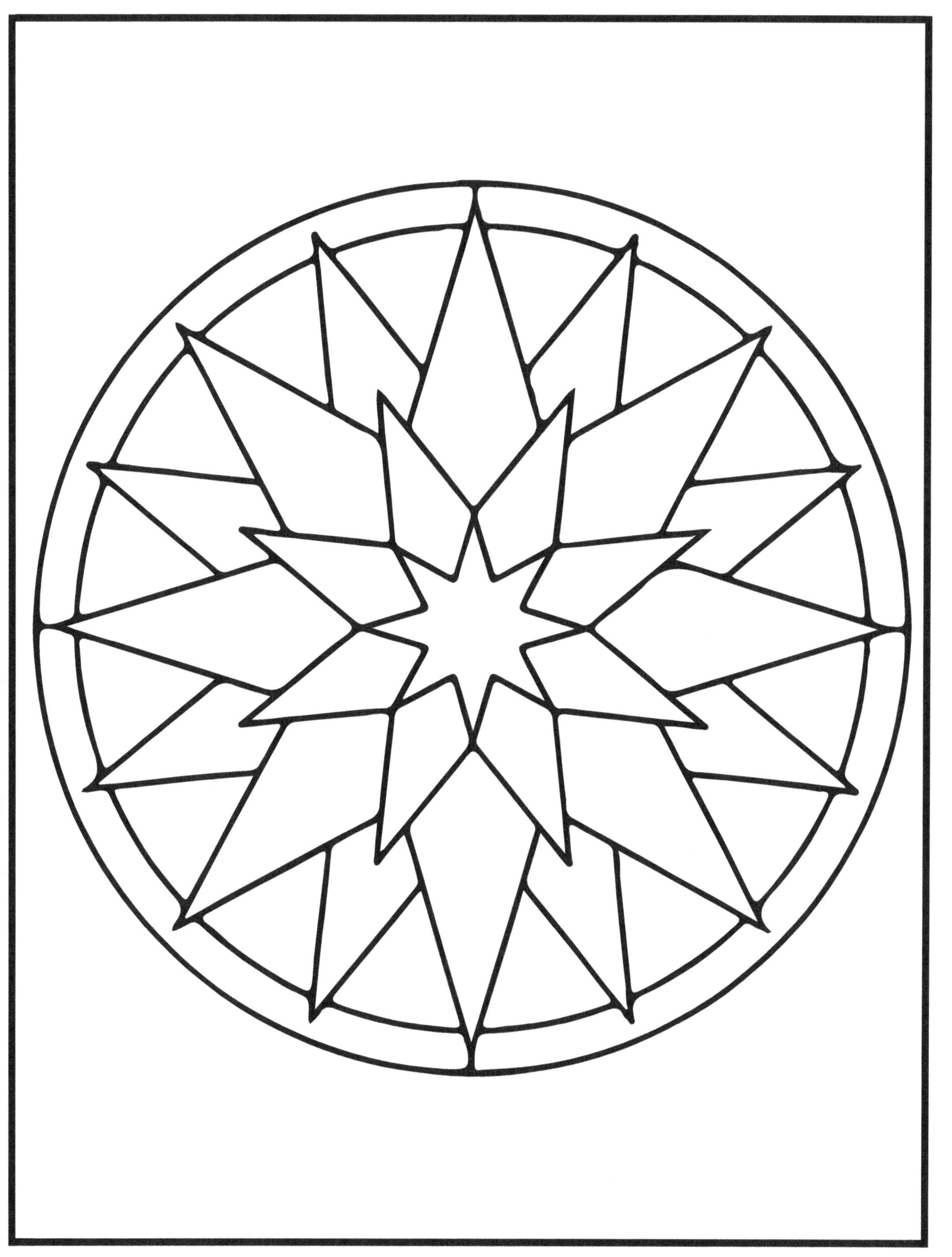

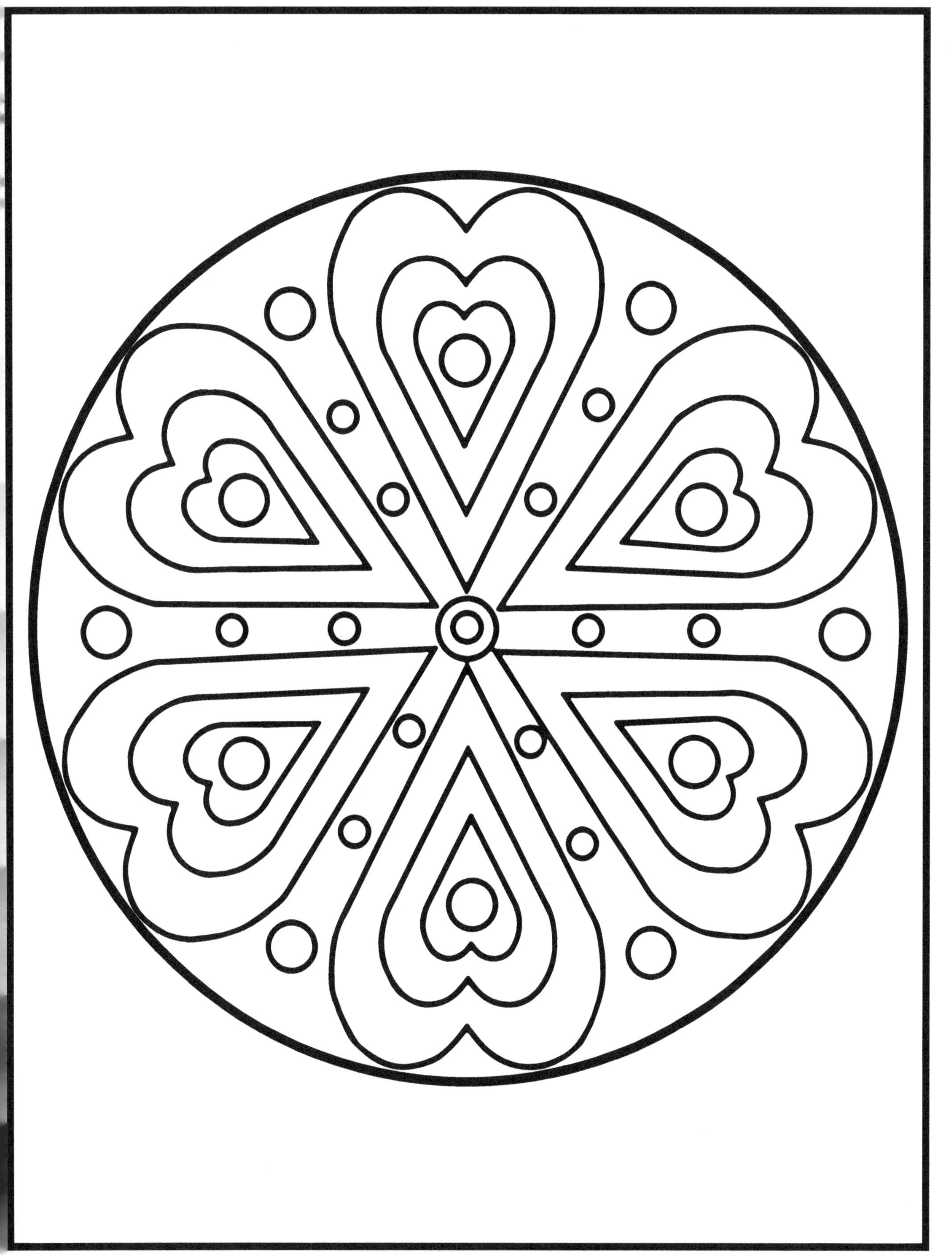

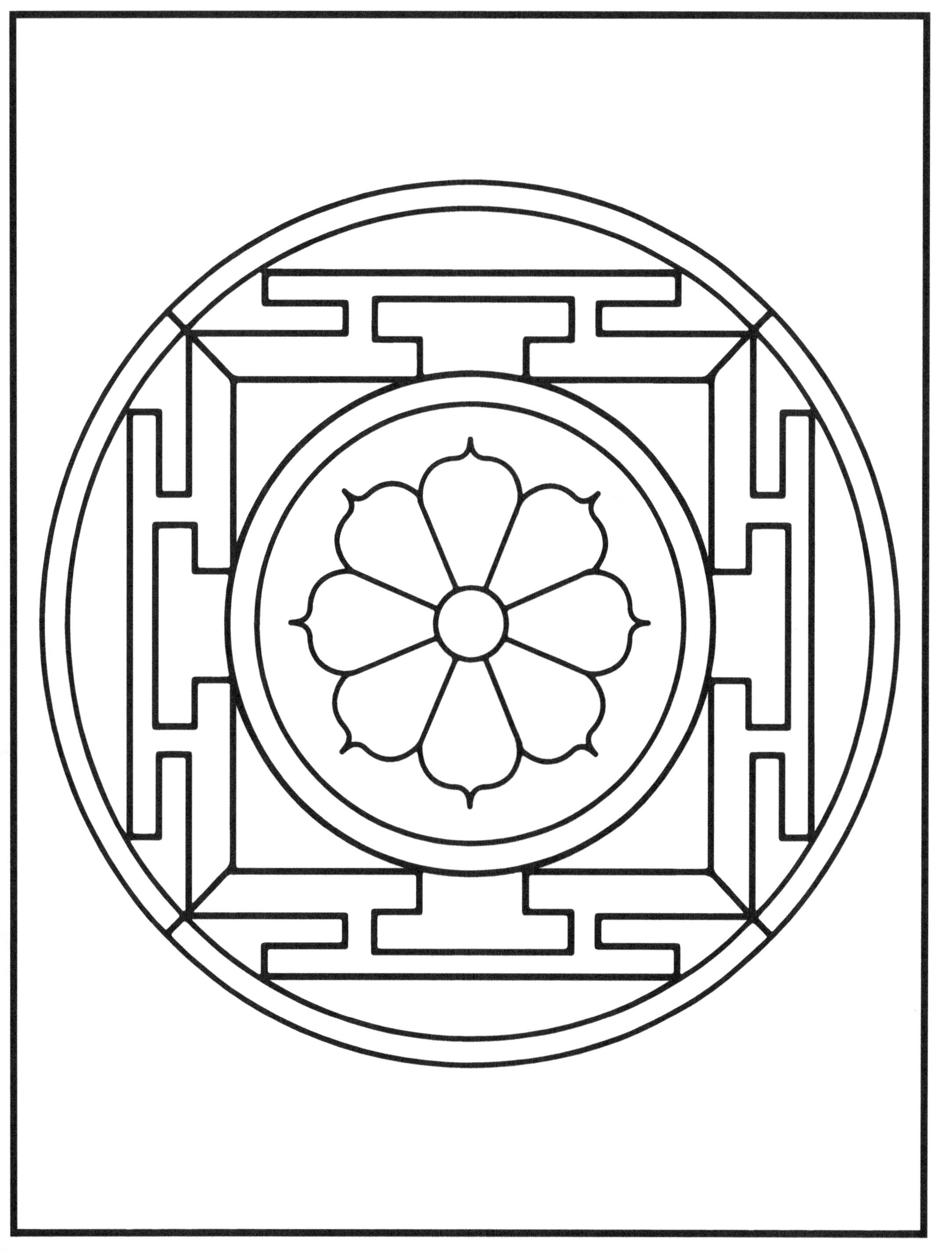

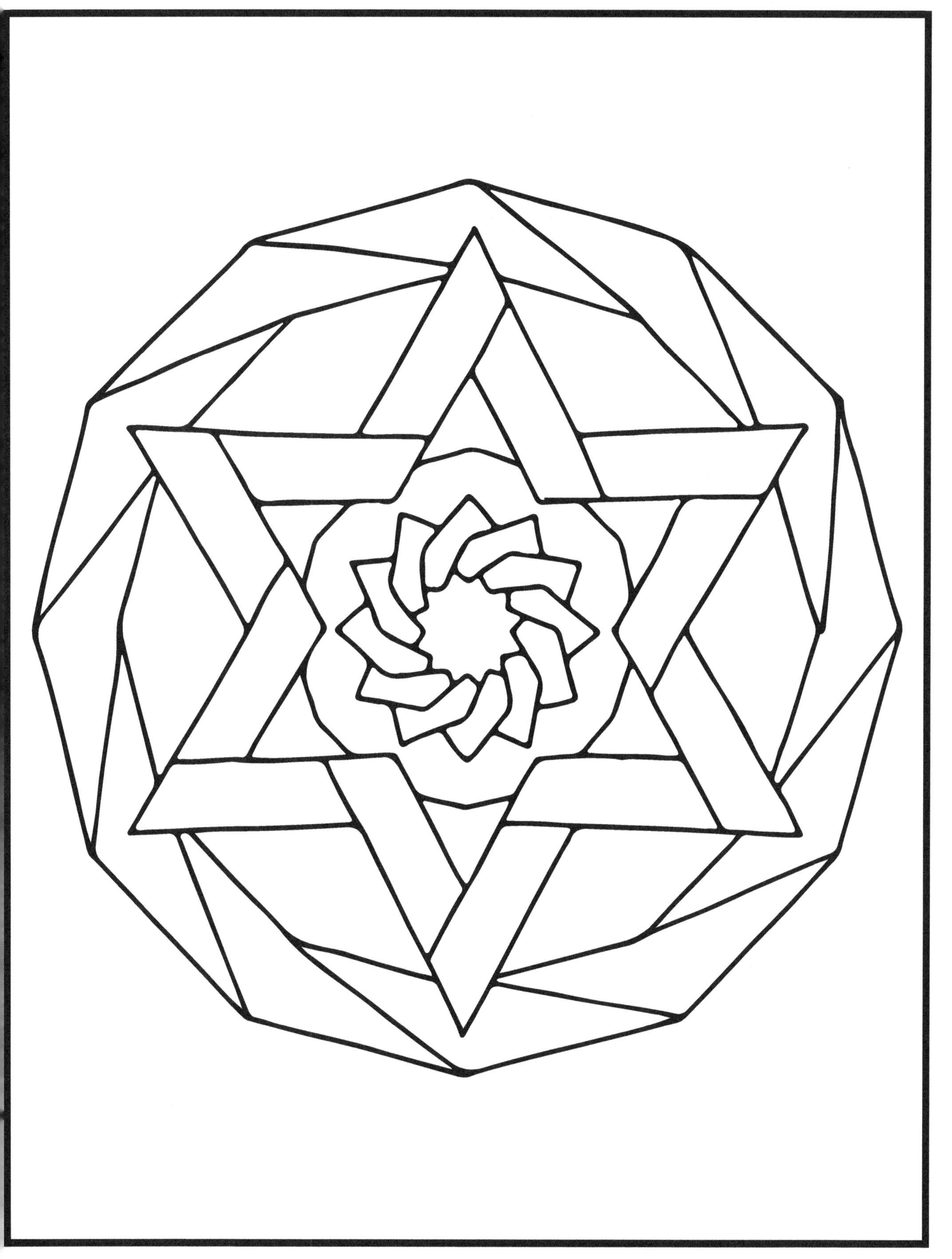

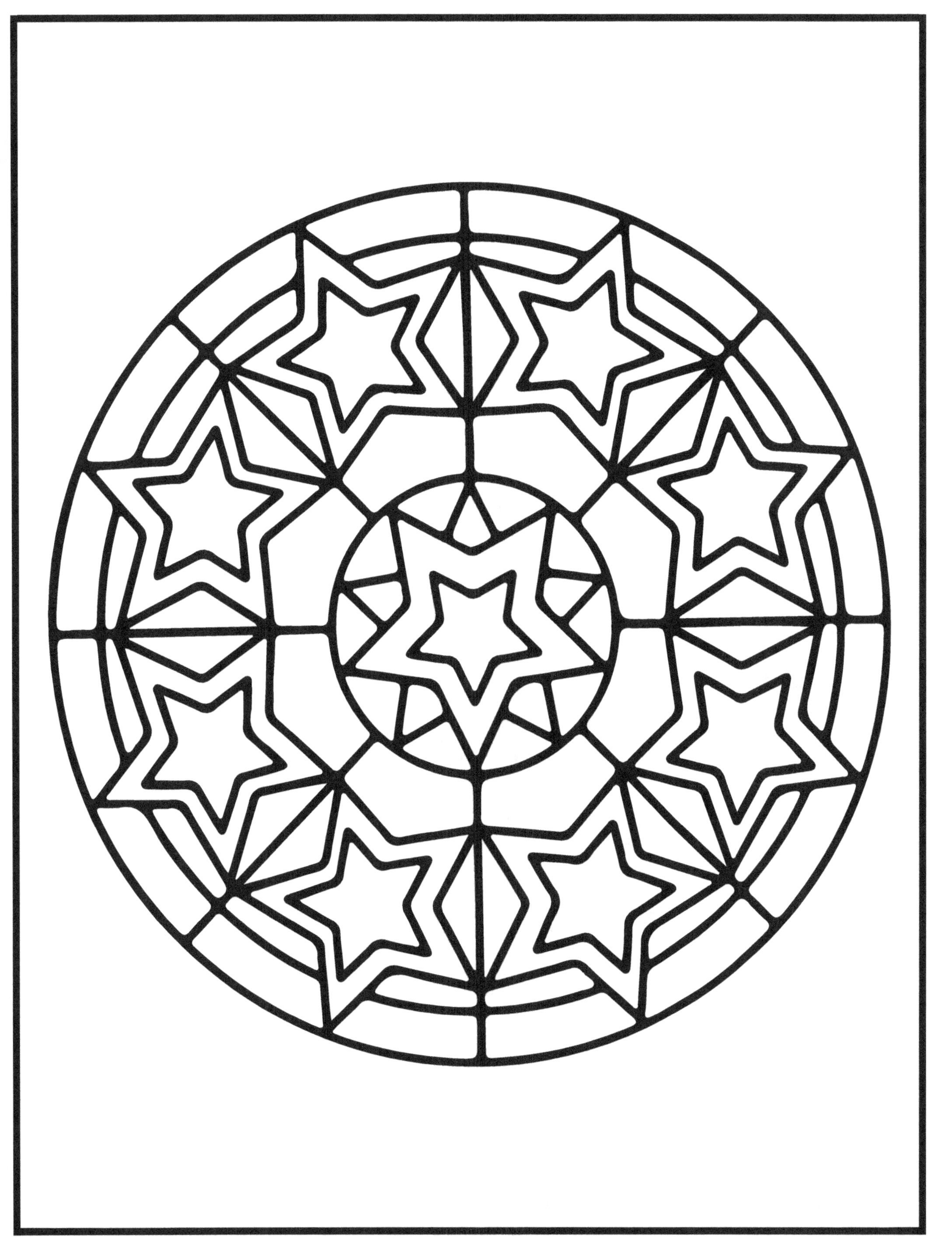

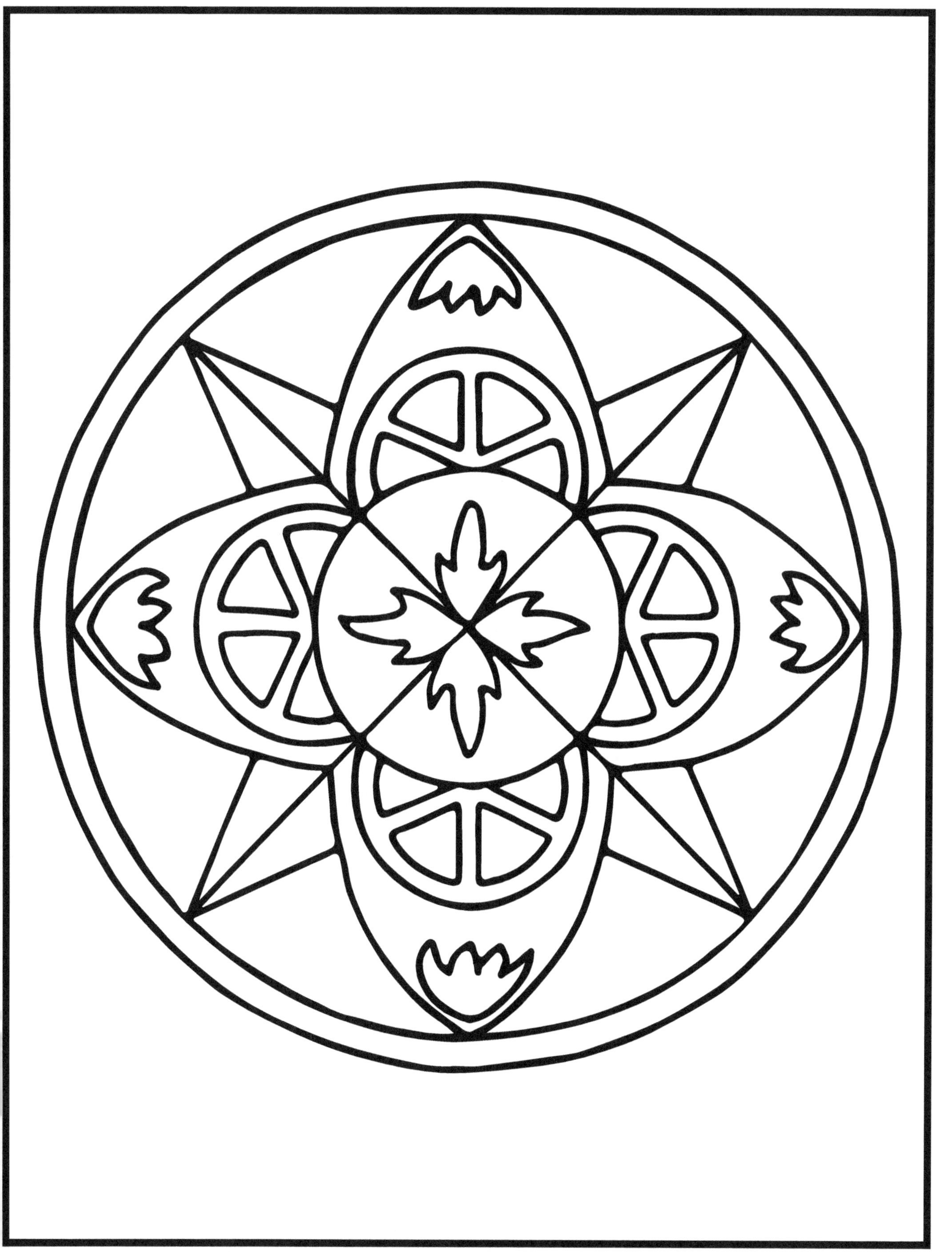

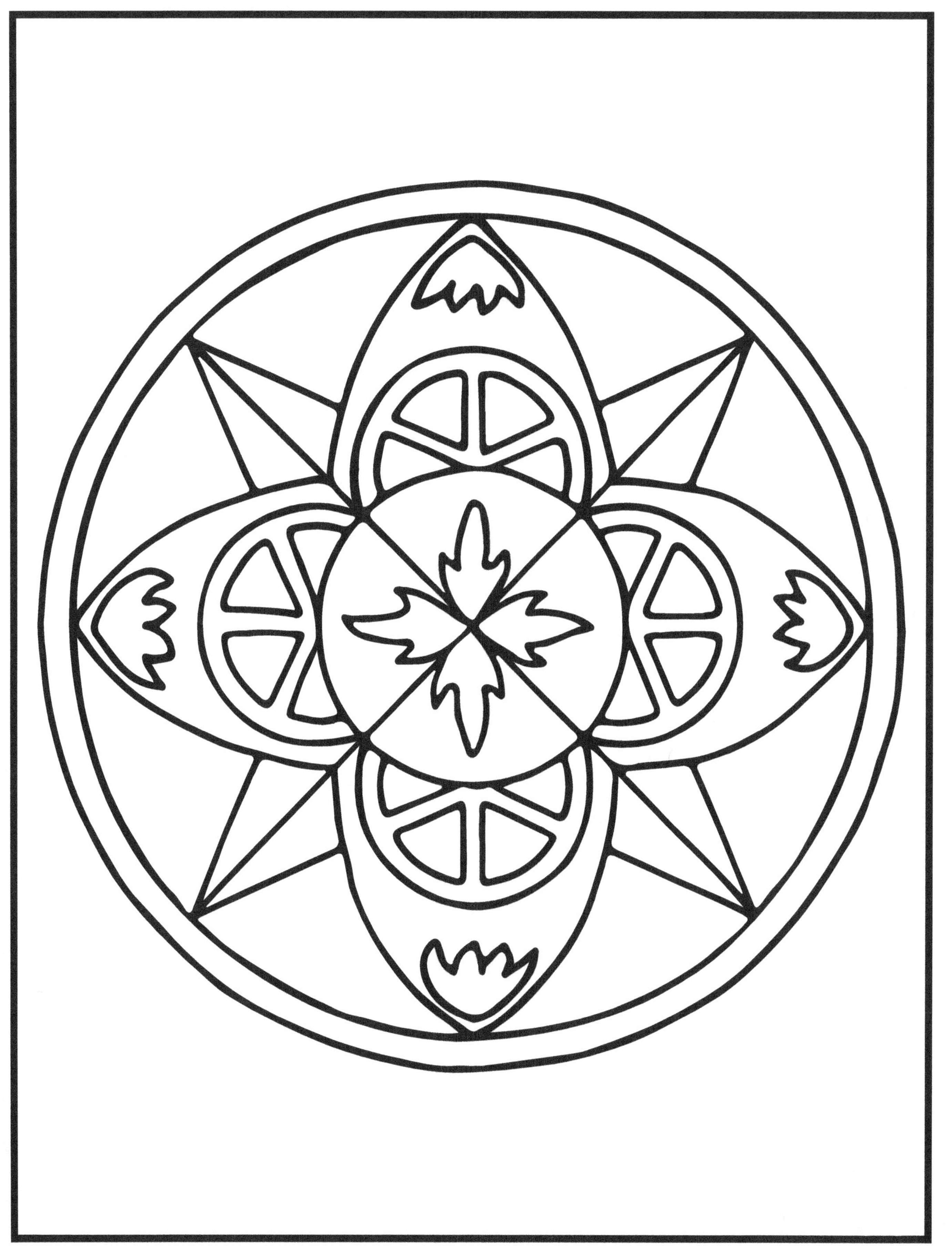

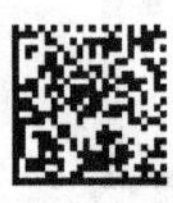